W9-AHK-333

Rome

0 — 500m
0 — 500yds

TYRRHENIAN SEA

0 — 20km
0 — 20miles

CONTENTS

ABOUT THIS BOOK

This *Step by Step Guide* has been produced by the editors of Insight Guides, whose books have set the standard for visual travel guides since 1970. With top-quality photography and authoritative recommendations, this guidebook brings you the very best of Rome in a series of 18 tailor-made tours.

WALKS AND TOURS

The tours in the book provide something to suit all budgets, tastes and trip lengths. As well as covering Rome's many classic attractions, the routes track lesser-known sights and up-and-coming areas; there are also excursions for those who want to extend their visit outside the city.

The tours embrace a range of interests, so whether you are an art fan, a history buff, a gourmet, a compulsive shopper, or have kids to entertain, you will find an option to suit.

We recommend that you read the whole of a tour before setting out. This should help you to familiarise yourself with the route and enable you to plan where to stop for refreshments –

Above: Temple of Saturn in the Forum; Cosmatesque floor in Santa Maria Maggiore; she-wolf suckling Romulus and Remus; staircase in the Vatican Museums; Castel and Ponte Sant'Angelo.

options for this are shown in the 'Food and Drink' boxes, recognisable by the knife and fork sign, on most pages.

For our pick of the walks by theme, consult Recommended Tours For… *(see pp.6–7)*.

OVERVIEW

The tours are set in context by this introductory section, giving an overview of Rome to set the scene, plus background information on food and drink, shopping and the city's museums. A succinct history timeline highlights the key events that have shaped the city over the centuries.

DIRECTORY

Also supporting the tours is a Directory chapter, comprising a user-friendly, clearly organised A–Z of practical information, our pick of where to stay while you are in the city and select restaurant listings; these eateries complement the more low-key cafés and restaurants that feature within the tours themselves and are intended to offer a wider choice for evening dining.

The Authors

Originally from Santa Fe, New Mexico, **Éowyn Kerr** has lived in Italy on and off since 1990. Trained professionally as a conservator and restorer of Italian Renaissance paintings, she contributes regularly to art history and conservation journal publications. Éowyn currently divides her time between London and Rome, where she teaches, lectures and leads in-depth walking tours of the Eternal City.

The excursions were written by **Annie B. Shapero**, a long-time resident of Rome and regular contributor to the Rome edition of *Where* magazine.

Margin Tips
Shopping tips, historical facts, handy hints and information on activities help visitors to Rome make the most of their time in the city.

Feature Boxes
Notable topics are highlighted in these special boxes.

Key Facts Box
This box gives details of the distance covered on the tour, plus an estimate of how long it should take. It also states where the tour starts and finishes, and gives key travel information such as which days are best to do the tour and handy transport tips.

Footers
Those on the left-hand page give the tour name, plus, where relevant, a map reference; those on the right-hand page show the main attraction on the double page.

Food and Drink
Recommendations of where to stop for refreshment are given in these boxes. The numbers prior to each restaurant/café name link to references in the main text. The restaurants/cafés are also plotted on city maps.

Restaurants/cafés are open daily, unless otherwise stated. The € signs at the end of each entry reflect the approximate cost of a two-course meal for one, with half a bottle of house wine. These should be seen as a guide only. Price ranges, also quoted on the inside back flap for easy reference, are as follows:

€€€€   €60 and above
€€€   €40–60
€€   €25–40
€   €25 and below

Route Map
Detailed cartography shows the tour clearly plotted with numbered dots. For more detailed mapping, see the pull-out map slotted inside the back cover.

HISTORY BUFFS

Explore the heart of Ancient Rome (walk 1) and the Colosseum (walk 2), or head out further afield to the well-preserved ruins of Ostia Antica (tour 18), the ancient burial sites of the Appian Way (tour 14) and the Etruscan tombs at Cerveteri (tour 16).

RECOMMENDED TOURS FOR...

CHILDREN

Head for the Villa Borghese Park (walk 7), where the kids will love boating in the Giardino del Lago, as well as the puppet theatre and zoo. The Explora Children's Museum is lots of fun too *(see p.19)*.

ART IN CHURCHES

The mosaics in the medieval church of Santa Maria in Trastevere are spectacular (walk 10), while Santa Maria del Popolo is packed with Renaissance masterpieces (walk 7).

CLASSIC CAFÉS

Drink in Rome's literary history at Antico Caffè Greco (walk 5). For spectacular views, try Casina Valadier in the Pincio Gardens (walk 7). For people-watching, try one of Trastevere's many cafés (walk 10).

PIAZZA LOVERS

Enjoy the Baroque grandeur and spectacular fountains of Piazza Navona (walk 3), take in the vast colonnaded square of St Peter's (walk 8), or, in contrast, pretty Piazza Farnese (walk 3). Piazza di Spagna (walk 5) is *the* place to see and be seen.

FOOD AND WINE

The Jewish Ghetto (walk 10) is where to find hearty Roman dishes. For a picnic try the food market at Campo de' Fiori (walk 3), or the family-run Volpetti, one of the best delis in the city (walk 11). The Castelli Romani route is a gastronomic delight (tour 17).

ROMANTIC ROME

Stroll amid the orange trees of the Parco Savello (walk 11), enjoy romantic views of terracotta rooftops from the pretty terrace of the Pincio Gardens (walk 7), or take a boat trip along the Tiber (walk 10). Alternatively head for the sumptuous gardens of the Villa d'Este in Tivoli (tour 15).

LITERARY TYPES

Visit the house John Keats lived in overlooking the Spanish Steps, now the Keats-Shelley Memorial House (walk 5). Pay homage to Keats and Shelley in the Protestant Cemetery where they are both buried (walk 11).

SHOPPING

Rome's most opulent shopping street is Via dei Condotti (walk 5), while an interesting mix of chic boutiques and studios can be found in the neighbourhood of Monti (walk 13).

FINE ART ENTHUSIASTS

An extraordinary collection of ancient art and statuary can be found at the Capitoline Museums (walk 1). Leave plenty of time for the Vatican Museums, especially Michelangelo's ceiling of the Sistine Chapel (walk 8).

OVERVIEW

An overview of Rome's geography, customs and culture, plus illuminating background information on food and drink, shopping, museums and history.

CITY INTRODUCTION

Few other places command the respect and awe of the visitor the way the city of Rome does. The multifaceted and layered nature of the modern city is as much a draw as the ancient monuments, Renaissance palaces and grandeur of the Vatican.

In the Detail
At every step you'll see something to catch the eye; a shady courtyard with a bubbling fountain, a flower growing between ancient marble ruins, a Baroque facade above a modern café. And there's a wealth of detail above eye-level, so don't forget to look up.

Rome has long been called the Eternal City. It is difficult to tell if the name refers to the city as the seat of the Roman Empire, as the heart of the Catholic Church, as the capital city of Italy, or as a major pilgrim destination. The layer upon layer of history certainly has an eternal feeling, but it is the continuously unfolding drama of the city that is its biggest draw.

Walking through the *centro storico* (historic centre), one is struck by the sheer size and grandeur of the buildings crammed into the narrow, winding streets. Romans somehow manage to live amid their history with a surprising degree of indifference while rushing about their daily lives, and this is something of the appeal of the city.

ARCHITECTURE

The disregard of the local population to their extraordinary surroundings has a natural explanation in overfamiliarity. Rome is a city standing on the shoulders of its predecessors: medieval churches rise from the remains of ancient houses; a Renaissance palace balances on top of the Theatre of Marcellus, standing next to 20th-century apartments. The shapes of streets and piazzas often echo the preceding architectural spaces, providing a sense of discovery at every turn.

Ancient and Medieval Rome

Though the shape of the city has developed over three millennia, there were several distinct phases of construction. A fair amount of ancient Rome was built between the 1st century BC and 3rd century AD. Many of the buildings in the centre have ancient ruins in their foundations. These were added to during the late medieval period when resources were limited.

With the return of the Papacy from Avignon in the 1370s, there was a renewed interest in construction and civic maintenance that lasted well into the Renaissance. After the restoration of several of the aqueducts, the addition of fountains and water features to public spaces became a Roman obsession *(see margin, p.12)*.

The Renaissance

A huge number of Rome's architectural gems date from the Renaissance (mid-15th to 17th century), when Rome was once again a cultural centre at the heart of Europe. This period saw major construction of palaces, roads, piazzas and churches, as each noble

family tried to outshine their neighbours. This was the age of the Baroque, perfected by Gianlorenzo Bernini – theatrical and bold, Bernini's Rome is an open-air gallery of fountains, façades and sweeping curves.

Unified Italy

Grand boulevards and huge public works buildings were not added until the post-Unification era of the 1870s. Again the face of Rome was permanently changed with the addition of floodwalls on the banks of the Tiber, the expansion of neighbourhoods, and the destruction of ancient ruins and medieval quarters to build 'modern' monuments and straight streets in the new capital city. This idea was picked up again under the Fascist regime of Mussolini, who wanted not only grand architecture to represent his ideals but also architecture to represent industry.

The 20th Century

Following World War II, vast neighbourhoods were rebuilt using cheap construction materials to provide inexpensive post-war housing. Sections of Rome damaged in Allied bombing raids were rebuilt, and restaurants and businesses were remodelled with the ubiquitous 1960s-era terrazzo floors, chrome and wood panelling.

The 21st Century

Exciting new additions have recently been made to the cityscape in the form of contrasting ultramodern architecture *(see feature box, right)*.

CITY LAYOUT

The face of the city is defined by its natural topography. Originally Rome was founded on the famous Seven Hills that sit on the left bank of the snaking Tiber River. The hills of the Aventine, Capitoline, Caelian, Esquiline, Palatine, Quirinale and Viminale and the valleys in between have been inhabited since at least 1000 BC. These areas still form the core of the city centre, but over the

Above from far left: statue in the Palazzo dei Conservatori; view from the top of the Spanish Steps; detail from the Fountain of Neptune in Piazza Navona; the Forum.

Modern Architecture

In a city dominated by its monumental past and traditional values, some of the best-known modern architects are daring to make their mark. Genoese architect Renzo Piano's state-of-the-art Auditorium, opened in 2002, spawned a wave of ultramodern architectural projects; these include Richard Meier's controversial new pavilion housing the Ara Pacis (an ancient Roman altar; *see p.42*), which, like it or loathe it, is a major new landmark on the cityscape; Zaha Hadid's ambitious new contemporary art centre (National Museum of 21st-Century Arts, known as MAXXI), nearing completion in the northern suburbs; and the Centrale Montemartini museum, an imaginatively converted electrical power plant in Ostiense housing part of the Capitoline Museums' vast collection of ancient statuary *(see p.75)*.

Still Waters

Some of the charm of Rome is the abundance of flowing water and decorative fountains. The early Romans built the great aqueduct system that supplied drinking water to the city. Fresh drinking water still runs freely for public consumption, and can be found in drinking fountains called *nasoni* (big noses).

Below: sunset over St Peter's and the Ponte Sant'Angelo.

ages Rome has expanded to include the Pincio Hill to the north, and the Janiculum Hill (Gianicolo) across the river. The *centro storico* is a relatively small area defined by the 3rd-century Aurelian Wall. Compact and walkable, it extends across the river to include Trastevere.

20th-Century Developments

In the early-20th century, new construction following Unification added districts such as Prati, the Via Veneto, Castro Pretorio, Salario and pretty Parioli. A great influx of population post-World War II further expanded the city in a middle-class urban sprawl, extending south along the Via Ostiense, and north to the *grande raccordo anulare* (GRA or ring road). The satellite city of EUR, or *Esposizione Universale*

Romana, was built as a Fascist-era utopia in the 1930s. Construction was halted with the fall of Mussolini, and the area has now been inhabited by several generations of Romans.

Port City

In the heat of summer, Rome does not feel like it is on the water, yet in many ways it is a port town. The nearby Ostia sits at the mouth of the Tiber floodplain, along a stretch of perfect Mediterranean beach. Ostia Antica was the major port of ancient Rome, bringing supplies up the river from all parts of the world.

The riverside atmosphere was inseparable from life in Rome, and up until a century ago inhabitants would hop in their skiff to fish or row across the Tiber. The city centre's watery feel changed dramatically with the construction of the floodwalls that now line its banks.

PEOPLE

Considering that Rome is the capital city of Italy it has a relatively low population. Around 2.7 million residents live in the city proper, with a total of four million in the greater metropolitan area. There is a general feeling of crowded sidewalks and noisy traffic, which is more indicative of the Italian culture than actual numbers of people.

Unsurprisingly, most of the city's inhabitants are Roman Catholic. However, in the recent past there has been an influx of legal emigration from North Africa, China, Southeast Asia, former Yugoslavia and Central America, which is changing the face of the population.

When in Rome

Rome has its own particular 'schedule', a pace that seems to defy all definitions of time management and practicality. This laissez-faire attitude often gives the impression that the Romans care little about the needs or time limitations of the visitor. The impression couldn't be further from the truth. Scratch below the surface of any Italian's seemingly indifferent façade and you will find a friend for life. The key to this lies in the immortal phrase, 'when in Rome do as the Romans'. Tourists and residents alike are simply expected to do what everyone else is doing. Insisting the local way isn't effective is generally met with a cold shoulder. If you ask Romans why, they will simply tell you, *e cosi*, that's the way it is.

open, and the workday is arranged so that people can enjoy a bit of sun at lunch. Romans are known for their stylish skimpy fashion, designed with heat in mind. They are also famous for their architectural styles which make the best of the weather; balconies and rooftop terraces, shady courtyards and tree-lined piazzas.

Despite the eclectic look and chaos of the city centre it works surprisingly well. Romans still know how to live the good life, and they do it outdoors. After you have had a chance to see the sights, wander the streets, and get your fill of museums and churches, find a café terrace or spot on a piazza and sit and watch the ebb and flow of this great city under the deep blue of the evening sky.

Above from far left: wandering the atmospheric streets of Trastevere; church of Santa Maria del Popolo; Roman balcony; expect some queues when you visit St Peter's and the Vatican.

Below: the church of Trinità dei Monti overlooks the Spanish Steps.

CLIMATE

The climate is one of the main draws for visitors and immigrants alike. Rome has sunny weather for an average of 10 months a year. The winters can be cold and rainy, but temperatures rarely drop below 4°C (40°F). In contrast summers are long and hot, with an average of 20°C (68°F) from mid-May through to mid-October, with temperatures in July and August well above the European average high of 28°C (83°F).

A Life Outdoors

With the sunny warm days it is not surprising that life is lived outdoors. Restaurants are designed to spill out on the streets, windows are left wide

FOOD AND DRINK

The culinary traditions of Italy have been praised for generations, and any trip to Rome would be incomplete without trying some of the local delicacies. These include hearty pastas, delicate fish, grilled meats, deep-fried artichokes, and of course wine.

The Bill, Please
It is considered most courteous in Italian culture to let the diner enjoy a meal without feeling rushed. You may find yourself sitting for ages before anyone even looks in your direction. When you are ready to leave, simply request *il conto per favore* (the bill please).

Italy is a land of regional cuisines, and while the names of well-known dishes are relatively similar throughout the country, the flavours are distinct. Rome is no exception, and restaurants of all classes and prices will generally offer their favourite local dishes. The delight of the Roman dish is in the simple combination of ingredients and the way in which it is prepared.

ORDER OF THE DAY

Of course it is one thing to eat in Rome, and completely another to eat on the Roman schedule. Generally Italians eat a light breakfast of biscuits and coffee with milk. A mid-morning break is a must, and consists of a quick stop for a coffee and a *brioche* (sweet Italian-style croissant). Lunch is served between 1 and 3.30 or 4pm, and can be quite leisurely. The dinner hour starts at 8pm until 11.30pm or later. This can be a difficult adjustment for those used to eating earlier.

The Menu
Traditional Italian menus have five full sections. They are arranged in the order in which they should be eaten, and dishes are served with a slight pause between each course. The menu starts with the *antipasto* (appetizer), followed by the *primo* (first course), consisting of either pasta, rice or soup. Next is the *secondo* (second course), or the meat, fish or poultry dish. Salads or vegetables are listed under *contorni* (side dishes). Seasonal vegetables do not always appear on the menu but they are usually available, and salads are never eaten before the main courses.

You don't have to order all the courses. For example, a pasta *primo* could be followed by a salad served in place of a *secondo*. The final dish is of course the *dolce* (dessert), followed by a digestive liqueur or an espresso at the end.

PLACES TO EAT

Half the joy of Rome is to be found in its bustling restaurants, tiny cafés tucked between ancient monuments, and umbrella-covered tables spilling out into the streets. Food is a social event in this grand town.

Cafés or Bars
Cafés are generally referred to in Italian as *bar*, which is actually the counter where coffees are served. Rome has more than 8,000 bars in the historic centre, indicating their importance in the cultural and social fabric.

In addition to coffee, they often serve aperitifs, cakes and pastries, and sandwiches. There are two listed prices at cafés – one for standing, and the other for table service. You will generally need to pay first and bring the *scontrino* (receipt) to the bar before ordering.

Pizzerie, Trattorie and Osterie

The goal of the meal at an *osteria* or *trattoria* is good food not presentation, and they are often casual places. House wine is often served in litre or half-litre carafes. Traditional wood-oven *pizzerie* serving thin-crust pizzas are not open for lunch. A lunch version is available as *pizza a taglio* (by the slice), which is thicker and sold by weight.

Ristorante

Expect to find an elegant dining area with tablecloths and candle-lit settings. Rome's restaurants can be anything from tiny and charmingly old fashioned to Michelin-starred. Most will have excellent service and an extensive wine list.

HAVING A DRINK

Wine Bars

The great wines of Italy are generally available at any place where food is served. The best choices for wines are *enoteche* (wine bars), which often have extensive label selections and fantastic wines by the glass. They often open before dinner and serve light fare. Italians, like the French, prefer to drink less wine of a better quality. It is considered ill-mannered to be drunk in public.

Bars, Cafés and Clubs

A number of Irish bars, serving beers and spirits and open until 1am, cater to the university crowd and to foreign visitors. These and several other pub-like bars can be found in Campo de' Fiori and between Piazza Navona and the Pantheon. Clubs also serve mixed drinks and are generally open quite late. The best sections for ultra-cool music and mixed drinks are in the Testaccio area or along Via Ostiense, while the more mellow or sophisticated clubs can be found around Piazza Navona. In the warm summer months there are a number of open-air clubs in the parks, along the river, and at the beach in Ostia.

Above from far left: al fresco café; chef at work; menu; tomato and mozzarella salad

Below: bar and club near Piazza Navona.

Jazz Dinners

The Rome jazz scene has picked up in the past five years or so, and there are a number of top live jazz clubs offering dinner and music specials. All of them have full restaurants and bars. Consider booking a table, having a meal and staying all night for the show. Good choices are: Alexanderplatz in Prati (Via Ostia 9, tel: 06-397 42171), Big Mama in Trastevere (Vicolo San Francesco a Ripa 18; tel: 06-581 2551), and Casa del Jazz near the Celio (Viale di Porta Ardeatina 55; tel: 06-489 41208).

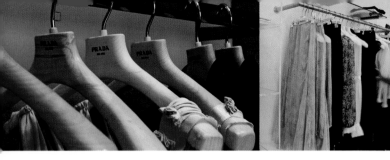

SHOPPING

Rome is that rare thing - a city on the international shopping circuit that somehow manages to keep small shops in business. While there is no shortage of fashion houses and divinely cool boutiques, there are very few of the ubiquitous high-street megastores.

Shopping in Rome still offers a few surprises if you have the courage to look. The most interesting shopping is found in neighbourhoods slightly off the beaten track, where you will find young designers, classic leather workers, made-to-measure tailors and other high-quality craftsmen, street markets and shops selling beautiful antiques.

MADE IN ROME

It is difficult to put a definitive stamp on what types of things are available in Rome. Leather goods, shoes, hand-made papers and books, art prints, kitchenware and antiques tend to be the best bet for good-value shopping in the city. Each area has a delicatessen offering a good selection of wines and enticing home-cooked food tucked into their windows.

Just as likely are the shops displaying strings of postcards and calendars, plastic heads of Caesar and cheap 'Venetian' glass made in China; though next to these you may also find the one-off shop with something that you won't be able to purchase in any other city. Several of the main districts can more or less be defined by their style.

Food Markets

A great place to pick up picnic provisions is at one of Rome's colourful food markets. The best known is on Piazza di Campo de' Fiori, but others include Piazza Mastai in Trastevere, Piazza dell'Unitá in Prati, and Piazza Testaccio. Markets are generally open Mon–Sat 7am–2pm.

WHERE TO FIND WHAT

Couture and Elegance

If real fashion-house fashion is what you are after then head for the Trident. The small streets crisscrossing between the triangle of the Via del Corso and the Via del Babuino are home to the big names in couture and international designers. Here is where you will find the latest creations by Chanel, Fendi, Roberto Cavalli, Brioni, Louis Vuitton, and the glittering jewels of Bulgari and Buccellati. Along the glamorous Via dei Condotti alone there is Gucci, Prada, Armani, Versace, Valentino and La Perla. The nearby Via Mario de' Fiori and the Via Bocca di Leone have some smaller but just as recognisable designers.

Chic Boutiques

Less elegant, less expensive and just as cool are Rome's boutiques. One-of-a-kind finds can be discovered in several locations. The newest player on the small designer scene is the neighbourhood of Monti. The shops along the Via del Boschetto are an interesting mix of slinky black dresses, cashmere in pretty colours, chunky arty jewellery, and stylish items for the home. The well-heeled Roman shopper can be

seen here picking up a fun new weekend frock.

Similarly, the streets near Piazza Navona and the Pantheon have a long-standing tradition of boutique style. Via del Governo Vecchio and the Via Campo Marzio both have their own distinct flavour, with funky designs and classic understated elegance. Trastevere is home to a good number of traditional tailors and ethnic or club-oriented shops.

High-Street and Mainstream

For shops like Benetton, Diesel, Miss Sixty and Zara there is always the jam-packed Via del Corso. Here you'll find all the familiar high-street names, high- and lower-end labels and all the books, music and trinkets you're after. Along its length is also one of Rome's few department stores, La Rinascente. This is located across from the Art Deco Galleria Alberto Sordi, which is essentially a small shopping mall.

A more pleasant version of Via del Corso is located in Prati, just a few streets away from the Vatican. The Via Cola di Rienzo is a wide boulevard lined with boutiques and cafés, the department store COIN and the speciality food shop Castroni.

For the younger crowd the Via dei Giubbonari, located between Campo de' Fiori and Via Arenula, is a great bet for inexpensive trends and the look of the minute.

Antiques

The Via dei Coronari is where to go for antiques. This elegant street has shops spilling out onto the pavement with some wonderful Italian furniture and paintings. In May and October antiques fairs are held here. The Via del Babuino comes in second for high-end pieces. For bargains the area of Monti has some good affordable finds, or real junk-hunting can be done at the Sunday Porta Portese street market in Trastevere (7am–2pm).

OPENING TIMES

In the touristy areas, most shops are open from 9.30am to 7.30pm. The larger department or chain stores will stay open through lunch (called *orario no-stop*), but family-run businesses and smaller shops mostly close between 1 and 3.30pm. Many shops close on Sunday and Monday, and very few stay open in August.

MUSEUMS

Rome is often referred to as the city of museums. At times the whole city seems like one vast open-air museum; nowhere else in the world is there such a varied collection of artistic treasures in such a compact space.

While some visitors are happy with a day spent picking through the ruins of the Roman Forum, imagining the gladiators at the Colosseum, or elbowing their way into the Sistine Chapel, many others will want to delve deeper into Rome's rich cultural heritage.

COMBINATION TICKETS

The City of Rome has set up combination tickets for some museums, providing substantial savings. The **National Roman Museum Card** (www.romaturismo.it) provides entry to all of the participating museums within a three-day period; these are the Baths of Diocletian, Palazzo Massimo alle Terme, Octagonal Hall, Palazzo Altemps and the Crypta Balbi.

The **Roma Pass** (tel: 06-8205 9127; www.romapass.it) is an excellent choice for savings. It comes as a kit, which includes a map, a three-day pass for unlimited bus and metro use, and free entry to two museums or sites of your choice, and reduced entry to many others. It also enables you to jump the queue at the first two sights you visit – especially useful at the Colosseum. Over 40 museums participate in the Roma Pass.

The **Roma Archeologia Card** (www.romaturismo.it) is valid for seven days and gives entry into all of the sites under the care of the Roman National Museums. These are the Roman Forum, Palatine Hill, Colosseum, the Baths of Caracalla, the Tomb of Cecilia Metella and Villa Quintili. A version of this is the **Appia Antica Card** valid for seven days for the Baths of Caracalla, Tombs of Cecilia Metella and Villa Quintili.

Tickets for the Capitoline Museums also include entry into the sister collection at the Centrale Montemartini (valid for seven days), while tickets for the Vatican Collections include entry into the Vatican Historical Museum at San Giovanni in Laterano, if used within five days of purchase.

ADDITIONAL MUSEUMS

There are number of wonderful, interesting or plain quirky museums not included in the walking tours. A selection of some of the best follows:

Archaeology

Crypta Balbi (31 Via delle Botteghe Oscure; tel: 06-678 0167; Tue–Sun 9am–7.30pm; charge). Combining state-of-the-art technology with dramatic ruins, this museum traces the development of Roman society.

Opening Times
As a general rule, State- and City-run museums are closed on Mondays. Private museums will often compensate for this by closing on either Sunday or Tuesday. Churches and the Vatican Museums are closed on Sunday. Opening times are seasonal and subject to last-minute changes, so it's worth checking in advance.

Case Romane (Roman Houses of the Celio Hill; Via Clivo di Scauro; tel: 06-7045 4544; www.caseromane.it; Thur–Mon 10am–1pm; charge, with advance reservation). More than 20 frescoes from the 2nd and 3rd centuries in a lovely museum space.

History

Museo della Civiltà Romana (Piazza Agnelli 10, EUR; tel: 06-592 6041; www.comune.roma.it; Tue–Fri 9am–2pm, Sat–Sun 9am–7pm; charge). This museum, tracing the history of Rome, is home to a magnificent model of Imperial Rome.

Museo Nazionale delle Arti e Tradizioni Popolari (National Museum of Folk Arts and Traditions; Piazza Marconi 8, EUR; tel: 06-592 6148; www.popolari.arti.beniculturali.it; Tue–Sat 9am–6pm; charge). A lively display of Rome's social history through folk art, costumes and more.

Fine Arts

Galleria Colonna (Via della Pilotta 17; tel: 06-678 4350; www.galleria colonna.it; Sat only 9am–3pm; charge). The Colonna collection rivals those of the Doria Pamphilj and Palazzo Barberini.

Museo Barracco (166 Corso Vittorio Emanuele; tel: 06-6880 6848; www. museobarracco.it; Tue–Sun 9am–7pm; charge). Palazzo Farnese, an elegant Renaissance palace, houses this prestigious collection of antique sculpture.

Palazzo Altemps (48 Piazza di Sant' Apollinare; tel: 06-3996 7700; Tue–Sun 9am–7.45pm; charge). Set around a courtyard, this delightful museum contains many treasures of Classical statuary and art from the Museo Nazionale Romano's collection.

Unusual Collections

Explora Children's Museum (Via Flaminia 82; tel: 06-3613 776; www. mdbr.it; Tue–Fri 9.30am–7.45pm; charge). Bring the children here when they are tired of ancient Rome; lots of buttons to press and levers to pull.

Museo Nazionale degli Strumenti Musicali (Museum of Musical Instruments; Piazza Santa Croce in Gerusalemme 9; tel: 06-7014 796; www.strumentimusicali.it; Tue–Sun 8.30am–7.30pm; charge). A small and interesting collection of rare or historically valuable instruments.

Above: ornate corridor ceiling in the Vatican Museums.

On the Periphery

There are several dynamic non-touristy spaces just outside the city centre. Located in the Flaminia area, northwest of the Villa Borghese park, is the Parco della Musica (Auditorium Parco della Musica; Viale Tiziano, www.auditorium.com), the spectacular music auditorium and concert hall in a building that resembles a giant armadillo.

Nearby is MAXXI (National Museum of the 21st-Century Arts; Via Guido Reni; www.darc.beniculturali.it/MAXXI), Rome's dramatic new contemporary art space.

In the same area, but across the river, is the Olympic stadium and Foro Italico sports complex, along the Via Foro Italico. The huge stadium is the main arena for AS Roma and SS Lazio football matches. This facility retains its Fascist-era decoration.

All three can be reached by taking the metro to Flaminio, and then catching tram no. 2.

HISTORY: KEY DATES

Emperors and popes, dictators and rebels, philosophers and barbarians, saints and sinners; from immense wealth to pillage and ruin, Romans really have seen it all.

FOUNDING OF THE REPUBLIC

753 BC	According to legend, Romulus founds Rome.
509	Fall of the seventh Etruscan king, Tarquinius Superbus. Republic established.
450	Roman law is codified.
390	Gauls plunder Rome.
312	Appius Claudius starts the Appian Way.
241	Victory in the First Punic War.
218	Second Punic War. Hannibal crosses the Alps.
146	Carthage and Corinth destroyed.
133	Civil war starts with the murder of Tiberius Gracchus.
100	Birth of Julius Caesar.
71	Gladiator revolt led by Spartacus ends in bloodbath.
60	First triumvirate: Caesar, Pompey, Crassus.
51	Julius Caesar conquers Gaul, crosses the Rubicon.
44	Caesar assassinated.
43	Second triumvirate: Antony, Octavian, Aemilius Lepidus.
31	Caesar Octavian Augustus defeats Mark Antony at Actium.

Above: Colosseum; Julius Ceasar; Baths of Caracalla.

THE ROMAN EMPIRE

Decline of Rome
Around 100 AD, Rome's population was well over one million; by 600 AD it had no more than 20,000 inhabitants, living among the ancient ruins and using them as a quarry.

27 BC	Caesar Augustus assumes autocracy, establishes Pax Romana.
41 AD	Caligula assassinated. Claudius accedes.
64	Great fire, and first persecution of Christians under Nero.
67	St Peter martyred.
80	Construction of Colosseum.
98	Empire expanded to Persia under Trajan.
125	Construction of Pantheon under Hadrian.
270	Aurelian builds defensive walls.
286	Diocletian divides empire between east and west.
312	Constantine defeats Maxentius. Establishes Christianity.
330	Constantinople made new capital of the empire.
410	Rome plundered and aqueducts destroyed under Alaric the Goth.

MEDIEVAL ROME

476	Last western emperor abdicates. Byzantium becomes seat of Empire.
590	Pope Gregory the Great instates papal protection.
800	Coronation of Charlemagne as Holy Roman Emperor.
846	St Peter's sacked by the Saracens.
1300	Pope Boniface VIII establishes the first Holy Year.
1309	Clement V abandons Rome, and moves papacy to Avignon.
1377	Papacy returns to Rome under Gregory XI.

THE RENAISSANCE

1417	The election of Martin V ends 40 years of papal schism.
1503	Pope Julius II starts work on new St Peter's.
1527	The Great Sack of Rome under German and Spanish troops.
1555	Confinement of Jewish Ghetto.
1572	Gregory XIII begins restoration of the aqueducts.
1626	New St Peter's is consecrated.
1797	Napoleon Bonaparte makes Rome a republic, and exiles the Pope.

19TH CENTURY

1815	The Roman Church state is restored by Congress of Vienna.
1849	Revolutionary establishment of new Roman Republic.
1870	Rome becomes capital of newly unified Italy. City renovation begins.

20TH CENTURY AND MODERN ERA

1922	Fascists march on Rome. Mussolini becomes dictator.
1929	Lateran Treaty creates Vatican State.
1944	Allied troops liberate the city.
1957	The Treaty of Rome is signed – the foundation for a united Europe.
1960	Rome hosts the Olympic Games. Period of 'La Dolce Vita'.
1994	Tangentopoli corruption investigations within the government begin.
2000	Rome jubilee celebrates the start of Christianity's third millennium.
2001	Media magnate Silvio Berlusconi is elected Prime Minister.
2002	Introduction of the euro, replacing the lira.
2005	Pope John Paul II dies. Cardinal Ratzinger elected Pope Benedict XVI.
2006	Berlusconi loses power to Romano Prodi.
2008	Romans vote in a right-wing mayor for first time in 18 years. Silvio Berlusconi is reelected Prime Minister.

Above from far left:
Roman senate in session, by Cesare Maccari; a procession of cardinals during the election of Pope Pius II, 1458, by Pinturicchio.

Rome Looks Right
In April 2008, Romans voted in a right-wing mayor, Gianni Alemanno, overturning nearly two decades of rule by the left-of-centre. Alemanno's campaign focused on the desire of many Romans for increased security, a cleaner, less traffic-clogged city and a solution to the influx of illegal immigrants.

WALKS AND TOURS

CAPITOLINE HILL AND ROMAN FORUM

The area between the Capitoline Hill and the Colosseum has been considered the civic centre of the Eternal City for thousands of years. This walk covers some of Rome's most important museum collections, then follows the Via Sacra through the city's oldest neighbourhood to Trajan's Markets.

DISTANCE 4.5km (2¾ miles)
TIME A full day
START Piazza Venezia
END Trajan's Markets
POINTS TO NOTE
While this walking route is actually quite contained there is a lot to see. There are few places to stop for a break along the way so a bottle of water and good walking shoes are recommended.

If all roads lead to Rome, then all roads in Rome seem to lead to **Piazza Venezia**, the hub of the city's road network since 1881. From the foot of the bombastic **Monumento a Vittorio Emanuele II** *(see box, p.26)* walk south along the Via del Teatro di Marcello and walk up the second stairway on the left.

Below: the she-wolf suckling Romulus and Remus.

CAMPIDOGLIO

The harmonious **Piazza del Campidoglio ❶** is located at the top of the Capitoline Hill, which rises majestically above the nearby Forum and city centre, and was once home to the important temple of *Jupiter Optimus Maximus*

Capitolinus. The ancient Tabularium (office of records and archives) built in 78 BC stands at the south side of the piazza in what is now called the **Palazzo Senatorio**. It still houses the city records offices of the local government.

Michelangelo's Design

The current look of the piazza dates from the Renaissance and is primarily the design of Michelangelo. Pope Paul III Farnese commissioned the remodelling of the space in celebration of the visit of Holy Roman Emperor Charles V, scheduled for 1538. His plan included the reworking of the grand stairs and the piazza to showcase the equestrian statue of Marcus Aurelius of 80 AD (an excellent copy stands in the piazza), while Michelangelo changed the orientation of the government buildings by turning them away from the classical Forum to face the Vatican. The two elegant palaces on either side of the piazza house the important collections of the Musei Capitolini.

Capitoline Museums

The entrance to the **Musei Capitolini ❷** (Piazza del Campidoglio 1; tel: 06-

8205 9127; www.museicapitolini.org; Tue–Sun 9am–8pm; charge) is on the southwest side of the piazza in the **Palazzo dei Conservatori**. It is considered the oldest public sculpture collection in the world and was founded in 1471 by Pope Sixtus IV (better known for commissioning the Sistine Chapel). The palace courtyard contains the remains of a colossal statue of Emperor Constantine. On view in the first-floor galleries are some of Rome's most famous treasures, including the statue of the 5th

Above from far left:
Marcus Aurelius in the Piazza del Campidoglio; looking out from the piazza; fragments of a statue of Constantine in the Palazzo dei Conservatori.

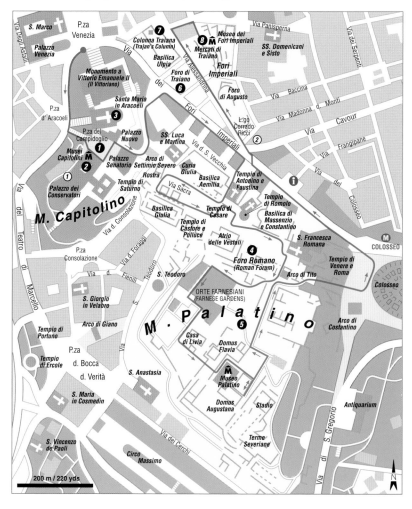

Above from left:
Il Vittoriano, or the 'Typewriter'; two scenes from the steps of Santa Maria in Aracoeli; Temple of Antoninus and Faustina.

century BC she-wolf suckling the infants Romulus and Remus, the classic *Thorn Puller*, and the Emperor Commodus posing as *Hercules*. Many of the rooms are highly decorated with works by Pietro da Cortona and frescoes by Cavaliere d'Arpino. The upper-level galleries showcase paintings by Guido Reni, Caravaggio, Tintoretto, Titian and Veronese.

Take the underground passage through the Tabularium, to the **Palazzo Nuovo** collection on the opposite side. Here are some of the best examples of ancient sculpture. The original *Marcus Aurelius* is in the courtyard. On the first floor are singular statues including a *Discus Thrower*, the *Dying Gaul* copied from a 3rd-century BC original, and the luscious *Capitoline Venus*. The rare collection of portrait busts of both emperors and philosophers is displayed chronologically.

'The Typewriter'

The massive monument of 'Il Vittoriano' on the Piazza Venezia, inaugurated in 1911, was intended to honour the newly unified Italy but is actually dedicated to the first King of the Republic, Victor Emmanuel II. Its construction was fraught with controversy as large sums of the newly imposed national taxes were funnelled into the project, and sections of the ancient Capitoline Hill and surrounding neighbourhoods were demolished to create space. Italians refer to the monument by derogatory names such as the 'wedding cake' or 'the typewriter'. The immense structure is topped by an oversized bronze equestrian figure of the king, and the Eternal Flame of the Fatherland and the Tomb of the Unknown Soldier are located on the front step.

If refreshments are needed there is a nice **museum café** inside the Palazzo Caffarelli, behind Palazzo dei Conservatori see ⑪①. It can be reached through the museum. The food is nothing special but the location and views are stellar.

Santa Maria in Aracoeli

Sharing the top of the Capitoline Hill is the 12th-century church of **Santa Maria in Aracoeli ③**. A long staircase, to the north of Michelangelo's grand stairway, leads to this jewel-like church. The climb up is worth the effort for a look at the interior, with oil lamps, sparkling mosaics, Cosmati floors, and 22 unmatched columns taken from nearby pagan temples.

ROMAN FORUM

Take the street at the left of Palazzo Senatorio to descend the Capitoline. From here there are sweeping views over the area generally referred to as the **Foro Romano ④** (Roman Forum). The main Forum sits in the valley created by the Palatine, Esquiline and Capitoline hills and served as the political, civic and religious centre of ancient Rome for a period lasting over a thousand years. Rome became a republic in 509 BC and the last monument to be erected in the area was the Column of the Byzantine Emperor Phocas added in 608 AD. The majestic remains of the Roman Empire still dominate the centre of Rome, even in their current form as a heavily visited archaeological park.

Sacred Way

To enter the site walk down the hill to the Via dei Fori Imperiali *(see margin, p.29)* to the **main entrance** of the Roman Forum and Palatine Hill (Via dei Fori Imperiali, the official office is at Piazza Santa Maria Nova 53, entrances also at Via di San Gregorio 30 and the Colosseo; tel: 06-3996 7700; www.pierreci.it; 8.30am–1hr before sunset; charge; tickets are valid for two days for the Forum, Palatine Hill and Colosseum). If there is a queue try the ticket area on Via di San Gregorio and start from the Palatine Hill.

What looks like a disorderly collection of ruins was once a magnificent city of temples, shops, courts and triumphal arches, connected by broad streets. The area survived several major restructures, and the additional Imperial Fora extended to the Forum of Caesar, Forum of Augustus, and the expansive Forum of Trajan. Entering the site along the **Via Sacra** (Sacred Way), takes you through the middle of the archaeological area of the Roman Forum.

Senate House

To the right of the main entrance, heading northwest along the Via Sacra, are the remains of the **Basilica Aemilia**, a massive 2nd-century BC meeting hall for traders and commerce. Just past it is the **Curia Giulia** (Senate House) designed to hold up to 200 senators. The original 7th-century BC structure was rebuilt four times after it was destroyed by fire. The current structure dates from 283 AD under the Emperor Diocletian. Some original decoration

remains, and the bronze doors were removed in the 17th century. They can be seen on the front of the Basilica of San Giovanni in Laterano *(see p.77)*.

Arch of Septimius Severus

The path leads past the triumphal **Arco di Settimio Severo** (Arch of Septimius Severus) constructed in 203 AD. The triple arch was built in celebration of the victory over the Parthians (Persians) and still displays carved reliefs depicting scenes from the battle. Across

---

Food and Drink 🍴
① **CAFFE CAPITOLINO**
Palazzo dei Conservatori on the Caffarelli Terrace; tel: 06-6919 0564; 9am–7pm; €
The museum café is located on an outdoor terrace with superb views. It is perfect for a quick bite, and coffee or tea. Inside is additional seating with more substantial food.

Below: view of the Forum from the Palatine Hill.

Imperial Fora
The remains of the Fori Imperiali lie on either side and buried beneath the Via dei Fori Imperiali. As Rome grew in power, its population increased and the original Roman Forum was no longer big enough to serve the city's needs. The Imperial Fora were built by a succession of emperors from Caesar to Trajan.

Below: details from the Palatine Hill.

from the arch is the **Rostra** (Speaker's Platform), built for public announcements *(see margin, p.27)*.

Temple of Saturn

Nearby are the massive Ionic columns with a section of frieze. It is all that remains of the **Tempio di Saturno**, first built in 498 BC to house the *Aerarium* (state treasury), and was the most venerated temple in the Forum.

The flat area with column bases is the **Basilica Giulia**, home to the civil courts. Some of the steps still have the remnants of games of marbles inscribed in the stone. On the far side you will see three fluted columns from the **Tempio di Castore e Polluce** (Temple to Castor and Pollux), next to an unassuming metal roof marking the **Tempio di Cesare** (Temple of Caesar). It was here that the great leader's body was brought after his death.

Temple of Antoninus and Faustina

Back along the Via Sacra you will pass the **Tempio di Antonino e Faustina** (Temple of Antoninus and Faustina), which was converted into a church in the 12th century with a Baroque facade extending into the portico space. Beyond is the circular **Tempio di Romolo** (Temple of Romulus) with its magnificent original bronze doors from 309 AD. The temple was likely part of the Forum of Peace, and was incorporated into the early Christian church of Saints Cosmos and Damian. The interior can be seen from the church (on Via dei Fori Imperiali). Opposite the doors is the path to the **Atrio delle Vestali**

(House of the Vestal Virgins) with the colonnade of the courtyard and the circular temple. Here the Vestal Virgins kept the sacred flame of Rome burning.

Just up a low hill are the massive brick remains of the **Basilica di Massenzio e Constantino** (Basilica of Maxentius and Constantine), dating from 303. The three arches indicate only the side section of the structure dominating the skyline.

Arch of Titus

At the far end of the Via Sacra is the **Arco di Tito** (Arch of Titus). The triumphal arch was constructed to mark the sack of Jerusalem in 70 AD by the forces of Vespasian and Titus. The carved reliefs depict the figure of Roma with Titus, and a distinct processional of the spoils of the war. The treasures include the altar and Menorah from the temple of Solomon.

Palatine Hill

Next to the Arch of Titus is the entrance to the **Monte Palatino** ❺ (Palatine Hill), the oldest inhabited part of Rome. Supposedly it was on the Palatine that the twins Romulus and Remus were found in the cave of the Lupercal (She-wolf). This green space has long been home to stylish Romans and the remains of numerous palaces can still be found. The panoramic hillside housed the likes of Caesar Augustus, Cicero and Marc Antony. Much of the Palatine was reworked in the Renaissance when it was purchased by Cardinal Alessandro Farnese and turned into an elaborate garden.

The **Orte Farnesiani** (Farnese Gardens) dominate the central area of the hill. Here a subterranean vaulted passageway leads to the **Casa di Livia** (House of Livia), the best preserved house in the Forum area.

South of the gardens lies the **Domus Flavia**, built by Emperor Domitian. The grey building sandwiched between this and the **Domus Augustana** is the **Museo Palatino** (same hours as main complex), housing a large collection of artefacts from the ongoing excavations. Nearby is the **Stadio** (Stadium), and beyond are the ruins of the **Terme Severiane** (Baths of Septimius Severus), complete with aqueducts. Below is the **Circo Massimo** (see p.33–4).

Exit the Palatino and Forum Romanum from the Via Sacra at the Colosseum. Tickets will allow entry into this section of the archaeological site for two days (see p.30). To continue the walk, take the Via dei Fori Imperiali, past the Visitors Information Centre along the right, to the Via Alessandrina.

If a break is needed there are a few places along the nearby Via Cavour. Generally the restaurants close to the Forum are overpriced, but try the **Enoteca Cavour 313**, see ⑪②.

TRAJAN'S FORUM

The raised walk makes a nice path above the remains of the **Foro di Traiano ❻** (Trajan's Forum). This monumental complex, started by Emperor Trajan in 106, extended along the Quirinale to the Capitoline Hill. Sections of the exedra are still visible along the arched curve of the lower markets. The remains of the basilica Ulpia can be seen on the left, and at the far end is the **Colonna Traiana ❼** (Trajan's Column).

This 38-m (125-ft) high victory symbol was erected in 113 in honour of Trajan's triumph over the Dacians. The column is in excellent condition given its age, but the original painted details have been lost. The elaborate relief carving depicts scenes from the battle, spiralling 23 times around the column from the ground upward. The inside is hollow and has a staircase leading up to the terrace. The statue of St Peter was added in 1587, replacing the original bronze of Trajan. The Emperor's remains were placed in the base of the column after his death.

Trajan's Market

Walk up the nearby stairs to the Via IV Novembre, the entrance of the **Mercati di Traiano** and **Museo dei Fori Imperiali ❽** (Trajan's Market and Museum of Imperial Fora; Via IV Novembre 94; tel: 06-679 0048; Tue–Sun 9am–7pm; charge). Here, you can walk along the old stalls which sold wines, seafood, vegetables, fruit and oil. The lower floors had space for offices and granaries, and even a tavern.

Above from far left:
Trajan's Market;
Palatine Hill.

Mussolini's Fora
The traffic-clogged Via dei Fori Imperiali is a fairly recent addition to the landscape. In 1932 Mussolini bulldozed medieval districts, Renaissance towers, and vast sections of the Fora in order to create a straight boulevard and orderly Fascist parade route.

THE COLOSSEUM

This route starts at the Colosseum, the enduring symbol of Rome, and makes a wide circle along the less visited side of the Forum to take in the grandiose remains of some of the city's best-preserved temples and monuments, located along the river.

Above: try and visit first thing in the morning to avoid the crowds.

Below: the defining image of Rome.

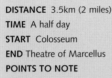

DISTANCE 3.5km (2 miles)
TIME A half day
START Colosseum
END Theatre of Marcellus
POINTS TO NOTE

Tickets for the Colosseum are now combined with the Forum and Palatine Hill, and can be used again within a 24-hour period. There are very few choices for food and drink between the Colosseum and the Circus Maximus, so consider packing a snack and a bottle of water for the first part of the walk. Children generally enjoy this route, although you may have to break it up as it is quite long.

THE COLOSSEUM

Incorporating some of Rome's oldest monuments, the walk starts outside the **Colosseo ❶** (Colosseum; Piazza del Colosseo; tel: 06-3996 7700; 8.30am–1hr before sunset; entrances also at Via di San Gregorio 30 and the Via dei Fori Imperiali; charge), in the Piazza del Colosseo, and continues to the far side of the Palatine hill.

The iconic amphitheatre was commissioned by the Emperor Vespasian in 72 AD to host the brutal but popular gladiatorial games and animal combat. Despite its condition it still remains an awe-inspiring sight.

History

The Colosseum was built over the site of Emperor Nero's artificial lake. Originally named the Amphitheatrum Flavium (Flavian Amphitheatre), it was given the popular nickname the Colosseum because of its proximity to the Colossus of Nero. The huge bronze and gilt statue once stood in front of the amphitheatre, reaching as high as the fourth floor. Part of the base of the colossal statue is still visible near the Via Sacra.

The ingenious design of the practical amphitheatre allowed for easy access of

up to 55,000 people, and the entire arena could be emptied of spectators in less than 10 minutes using all of the 80 arched entrances. The top of the Colosseum could be covered with a huge canvas awning shading spectators and contestants from the sun. However, the biggest draw of the Colosseum was not the architecture, but the games.

Deadly Purpose

The gladiator games and exotic animal fights were free of charge to the public. Events were often theatrical to lighten the gruesome nature of the real entertainment. The fights always ended in death and a constant supply of animals and men was needed to keep the system going. Gladiators were pitted against gladiators, animals against gladiator, and animal against animal. Around 5000 wild animals were slaughtered in the first 100 days of the games when the stadium first opened in 80 AD. While expensively trained gladiators were often spared death, animals and slaves never were. The brutal games were eventually banned in 523 AD.

Structure

What we now see from the main piazza are the skeletal remains of the once grand structure. The exposed brickwork is merely the inner support wall. Most of the magnificently carved decoration and massive block was stripped from the building and used for the construction of St Peter's and Renaissance palaces. The ransacking of

raw materials continued until the 18th century when Pope Benedict XIV consecrated it as a church. Major architectural reconstruction and restoration has been carried out in the last century to keep the building standing. Some of the decoration is still visible on the side facing the Via dei Imperiali.

How the Colosseum Worked

The view from the inside shows an open brickwork area under what was

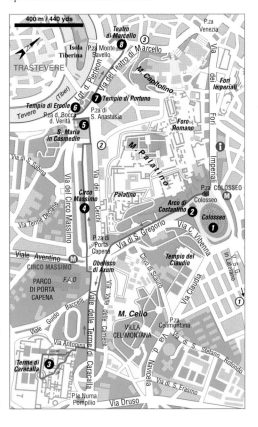

once a wooden-floored arena. The floor could be covered with sand and raked between games to 'clean' the arena, and it hid a series of trapdoors that opened to the rooms and animal cages below (now exposed). The seating is only visible in a few sections where marble block remains. Seating was organised in a complicated division of status and social class, and was often dependent on who was hosting the game. The best view of the internal structure is from the upper floors looking back down into the Colosseum. Exits are located at the north and west sides.

Rome vs Byzantium

When the Emperor Constantine I came to power in the fourth century the Roman Empire was already fragmented and overstretched. Constantine worked to unify some of the diversity in politics and religion, and established Christianity as an official religion at the Edict of Milan. At the time Christianity was seen as one of many mystical cults, and was much more popular in the east than in Rome. Constantine worked on spreading the Empire between two major cities, with Rome governing the west and Byzantium governing the east. He eventually moved the capital city to the more Christian-friendly Byzantium.

The new capital was renamed Constantinople (now Istanbul), and Rome was effectively left to decay. It was not long before the great palaces and temples were sacked by invaders.

If you're ready to eat now, take the north side exit and walk a few minutes east into the nearby neighbourhood of the Celio. Along the Via di San Giovanni in Laterano is the **Hostaria Isidoro**, see ⑪①, serving a great-value lunch or dinner.

To continue the walk follow the black paving stones from the west exit to the large Arch of Constantine, dominating the south side of the Piazza del Colosseo.

ARCH OF CONSTANTINE

The noble **Arco di Constantino ❷** is the last great triumphal arch to be constructed in the Roman Forum. It was erected in 315 by the Emperor Constantine I just before the shift of political power moved from Rome to Byzantium *(see box, left)*. Most of the magnificently carved decoration is made from 'recycled' scenes taken from other nearby monuments. The arch commemorates the Christian Emperor's famous battle against Maxentius at the Milvian Bridge, where he fought under the sign of the cross.

Towards the Baths of Caracalla

Walking past the arch along the Via di San Gregorio, and passing under a remaining section of aqueduct, you will come to an intersection at the Piazza di Porta Capena. Cross left at the lights, and continue along the tree-lined Viale delle Terme di Caracalla. Cross right at the Via Antonina and up the path to the entrance of the archaeological complex.

BATHS OF CARACALLA

The massive brick remains of the bath complex of the **Terme di Caracalla** ❸ (Viale delle Terme di Caracalla 52; tel: 06-3996 7700; www.pierreci.it; daily 9am–1hr before sunset, Mon 9am–2pm; charge) are a testament to what was once the world's largest leisure centre. Construction of the 11-hectare (27-acre) complex was started in 212 under the Emperor Caracalla. The baths, or *thermae*, were the ultimate statement of the architectural achievements of the Empire. The facilities could accommodate up to 1,600 people and in addition to the baths, saunas, gymnasia and massage rooms, there were spaces for lectures, shopping, art galleries and a comprehensive library. The largest rooms were the gymnasia.

Bathing Ritual

The important ritual of Roman bathing included first a dip in the hot caldarium, followed by the cooler tepidarium, then a plunge into the cold frigidarium, and finally a swim in the large pool, or *natatio*. Under the floor tiles was a massive labyrinth of water pipes, tunnels and heat conduits that were constantly maintained to keep the steam rooms and baths at the correct temperatures. The complex was used continuously for over 300 years, and was finally closed in 537 after the Visigoths sacked Rome and destroyed the aqueducts. Some of the matching sets of columns from the poolside portico can be seen holding up the nave of Santa Maria in Trastevere *(see p.71)*, and two of the great decorative basins now adorn the Piazza Farnese *(see p.40)*.

CIRCUS MAXIMUS

Exit left from the baths, continue northwest along the Viale delle Terme di Caracalla, passing the ominous looking FAO building (the Food and Agriculture Organization for the

Above from far left: snapshots of the Baths of Caracalla.

Below and far left: the Arch of Constantine.

Food and Drink 🍴

① **HOSTARIA ISIDORO**
Via San Giovanni in Laterano 59; tel: 06-700 8266; Sun–Fri noon–3pm, daily 7pm–2am; €
Built in a 17th-century cloister, this restaurant offers a rare combination – good food and excellent value near the Colosseum. You can tell the food is top notch because the restaurant is usually packed out with Romans. Try the tasting menu, or the wonderful seafood risotto; other classics include tagliatelle with artichokes and spaghetti with clams.

Below: the campanile of Santa Maria in Cosmedin.

United Nations); then cross the Viale Aventino and you will reach the **Circo Massimo ❹** (Circus Maximus).

Like many of Rome's ancient monuments the giant space of the circus is larger than legend. Dating back to the 6th century BC the grand outdoor arena hosted sporting events for nearly 1000 years. The original stadium held over 250,000 spectators, and the main attraction was the dangerous four-horse chariot race. The *spina* (centre spine) would have been raised and decorated with small temple-like structures and obelisks, attesting to the strengths and prowess of various athletes. Almost nothing remains of the original stadium structure, though green hillside at the left edge alludes to the seating. Some bits of brickwork at the southern edge are all that is left of the building.

Today the Circus Maximus is used as a public park and picnic area. It is perfect for an early morning jog or cycling with young children. Occasionally the space is still used for concerts and sporting events.

FORUM BOARIUM

Crossing the Circus Maximus, exit at the north corner of Via dell'Ara Massimo di Ercole and the Via dei Cerchi. You should find the delightful old-fashioned trattoria, **Alvaro al Circo Massimo**, see ⓪②, a great place for a traditional Roman long lunch or dinner.

Continue along the Via dei Cerchi, and turn left at the traffic-filled piazza. This low-lying area along the river is generally known as the **Forum Boarium** and was once used as the cattle market for ancient Rome.

Mouth of Truth

On the left is the church of **Santa Maria in Cosmedin ❺** (Piazza della Bocca della Verità; tel: 06-678 1419; daily 9.30am–6pm; free). Inside the covered entrance to the peaceful 6th-century church is the unusually popular **Bocca della Verità** (Mouth of Truth). There is often a queue as visitors are requested to leave a donation and approach the mouth one by one. This carving has a long history of use as a lie detector, dating back to the Middle Ages. Legend has it that if you place your hand in its mouth, and have not been completely truthful, your hand will be bitten off. The carving was likely originally made as a decorative manhole cover or drainage for a rain gutter. The Bocca della Verità was made popular in the 1953 film *Roman Holiday* starring Gregory Peck and Audrey Hepburn.

The church itself is pleasingly simple, with a nice mixture of

medieval and Romanesque decoration. The Cosmati floors are original, and at the far left there are some relics of St Valentine, always popular with young lovers.

Temples of Hercules and Portunus

Across the piazza are two lovely temples that are among the oldest in the city. The round temple dates to the 2nd century BC and is thought to have been dedicated to **Hercules** ❻. For many years it was mistakenly considered the temple of Vesta because of its circular structure. The roof addition is part of an ongoing restoration effort, but the columns are in remarkable condition considering their age.

The rectangular temple on the far side of the piazza is dedicated to **Portunus** ❼, the god who served as gatekeeper of the granary stores, and of the ports and harbours. The location of the temple along the Tiber banks is near the ancient market port, and it was likely erected in an auspicious position of protection. The temple is still set on its original base, giving a sense of the original height. The fluted columns and triangular pediment remain amazingly intact.

THEATRE OF MARCELLUS

The winding Via del Teatro di Marcello will bring you to the entrance of the **Teatro di Marcello** ❽ (Via del Teatro di Marcello 40; tel: 06-6710 3819; daily 9am–6pm; free). The once regal performance space of the theatre dates to the last years of the 1st century BC. It is named after Marcellus, the well-liked nephew of the Emperor Augustus who died at age 19. The area was originally cleared for construction by Julius Caesar. Ironically he was murdered in the nearby Theatre of Pompey before it could be built. The architectural plan was elegant and included three full seating levels *(see margin, left)*, holding 20,000 visitors.

Much of the decorative marble was removed to construct other buildings, and the empty spaces within the arches and supports were filled in with medieval buildings. The far side of the archaeological walk opens onto the main piazza of the Jewish ghetto *(see p.68)*, providing views of the opposite side. Nearby are three standing Corinthian columns that originally came from the Temple of Apollo in Greece.

Consider finishing the walk with a gelato or cold drink at the **Antico Caffè**, see ⑪③, a family-run business just opposite the entrance of the Teatro di Marcello, with umbrella-covered tables overlooking the theatre ruins.

Above: Circus Maximus and Palatine Hill.

Below: Bocca della Verità (Mouth of Truth).

Food and Drink 🍴

② ALVARO AL CIRCO MASSIMO
Via dei Cerchi 53; 06-678 6112; closed Mon; €€
This pleasantly old-fashioned trattoria serves a lovely selection of traditional Roman dishes with a homely atmosphere. It is generally packed with local government officials, and is best known for fish dishes and seasonal grilled porcini.

③ ANTICO CAFFÈ DEL TEATRO MARCELLO
Via del Teatro di Marcello 42; 06-678 5451; 7am–11pm; €
This family-run café makes fresh sandwiches daily. Try one of their excellent coffees, homemade pastries or a cold freshly squeezed orange juice, served at a street-side table.

PIAZZA NAVONA TO CAMPO DE' FIORI

The adjoining areas of Piazza Navona and Campo de' Fiori make two halves of the old medieval city centre. The winding streets still hold much of their charm, and open onto some of the most fascinating and picturesque squares in Rome.

DISTANCE 3.25km (2 miles)
TIME A half day
START Piazza Navona
END Sant'Andrea della Valle
POINTS TO NOTE

This route works well for either a morning or afternoon walk. The area is full of restaurants and cafés, making it easy to stop for a break and extend the walk to a full day. There is a lot to take in but the route is contained in a fairly small geographical area. Consider starting the walk in the early morning if you want to browse the fruit and vegetable market at Campo de' Fiori.

In Agony

The origins of the name Piazza Navona come from its use as a stadium. The shape of the Stadium of Domitian, with one end curved and the other straight, was designed for the original Olympic event of Greek-style footraces. It was referred to as the *piazza in agone*, or 'the place of the *agone*', meaning 'the site of the competitions'. Pronunciation of the word changed over the centuries to 'n'agone', and eventually 'navona'. The word is often misinterpreted as 'agony', particularly in reference to St Agnes who was martyred in Navona, and likely suffered in agony.

The tour starts with theatrical fountains on the grandiose Piazza Navona, and continues by exploring the surrounding neighbourhood, eventually arriving at the non-stop Campo de' Fiori, known for its exceptional morning market and night-time bars.

PIAZZA NAVONA

There is no other space in Rome that can rival the charm and appeal of

Piazza Navona. This pedestrian-only zone is filled with umbrella-covered tables, gelaterie, hawkers, gawkers, street performers, portrait painters, tourists and lovers. It is one of the few places where you can spot politicians munching sandwiches next to dog-walking pensioners, next to wide-eyed tour groups, all sitting under the shadow of a Baroque fountain.

History

The long thin floor plan of the piazza follows the layout of the ancient Stadium of Domitian from the 1st century AD. Domitian's sports stadium predates the construction of the Colosseum and was used for races and other 'agone' or games *(see margin, left)*. The seating could hold over 30,000 spectators and the stadium was in use as late as the 5th century. The current piazza echoes the seating area in the curve of the surrounding buildings.

The Fountains

The bold look of the piazza dates to the 17th century with the patronage of Pope Innocent X Pamphilj. Gianlorenzo Bernini started the fountain project in 1648 after weighting the

open competition for the commission in his favour. His magnificent plan for the **Fontana dei Quattro Fiumi** ❶ (Fountain of the Four Rivers) incorporated the obelisk from the Circus of Maxentius. Four continental rivers are represented by massive allegorical figures, providing a connection between the powers of the waters and the powers of the continents. Depicted are the Danube for Europe, the Ganges for Asia, the Nile for Africa and La Plata for America. The figures provide architectural supports to lift the massive obelisk above the waterfalls. Integrated in the composition is the papal insignia of Innocent X.

The two other fountains actually predate Bernini's centrepiece. These works are primarily by Giacomo della Porta from the late 1570s. The **Fontana di Nettuno** (Fountain of Neptune) is located at the north end, and the **Fontana del Moro** (Fountain of the Moor) at the south.

Sant'Agnese in Agone

Directly facing the Fontana dei Quattro Fiumi is the church of **Sant' Agnese in Agone** ❷ (Saint Agnes in Navona; tel: 06-6819 2134; Tue–Sun 9am–noon, 4–7pm; free) distinguished by its rolling concave facade. The exterior appearance of the church is the work of Bernini's rival Francesco Borromini. The church is dedicated to St Agnes, an early martyr who was publicly executed in the Stadium of Domitian in 304 AD, see margin.

The Baroque interior of the space is stunning. The high-relief side altars

complement the massive sculptural centrepiece depicting the Miracle of Sant'Agnese.

Palazzo Pamphilj

Before leaving Piazza Navona, have a look at the long palace at the left of the church. The **Palazzo Pamphilj** (not to be confused with the nearby Galleria Doria Pamphilj, *see p.45*) was once home to Pope Innocent X and, like the piazza in front, was decorated accordingly. It is now the seat of the Brazilian Embassy, but some of the great frescoes by Pietro da Cortona can be seen through the massive windows that look onto the piazza. It is tempting to stop for a meal on the Piazza Navona but much of the food is overpriced and of

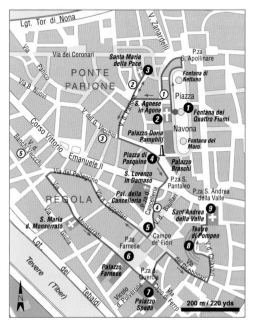

Agnes

Legend tells us that Agnes, a young virgin and devout Christian, refused an arranged marriage with a high-ranking member of the Roman, and therefore pagan, military guard. He ordered her publicly stripped in the piazza to force her to renounce her faith. Miraculously, her hair grew to protect her modesty. The guards then tried to burn her on a pyre, which also miraculously refused to light. She was finally beheaded.

Below: market stall.

low quality. Just a few streets off the piazza are some of Rome's best eateries.

Exit the piazza at the north end, past the Fontana di Nettuno, and turn left on the Piazza Sant'Apollinare. Directly on the left you will find a small open archaeological dig. Some of the entry arches and concession shops of the Stadium of Domitian are visible. Continue bearing left, past the triangular-shaped Largo Febo, which becomes Via Santa Maria del Anima.

At the corner is **Osteria del Anima,** see ⑪①. With outdoor tables and an excellent menu it is a favourite lunch or dinner spot for locals and tourists alike.

If you prefer a short break at one of the cool retro cafés then continue along to Via di Tor Millina and right to the Via della Pace. At the corner is the ever-popular **Antico Caffè della Pace,** see ⑪②, with its romantic ivy-covered facade.

SANTA MARIA DELLA PACE

Tucked into the end of the street, just past the Antico Caffè della Pace, is the little church of **Santa Maria della Pace** ❸ (Vicolo dell'Arco della Pace 5; tel: 06-686 1156; Tue–Fri 10am–12.45pm; free, charge for concerts), another hidden gem. The church, dedicated to St Mary of Peace, was started under Pope Sixtus IV in honour of a peace agreement forged with Turkey in 1482. Much of the space was remodelled by Pietro da Cortona. There are frescoes by Raphael, Rosso Fiorentino and Baldassarre Peruzzi. Perhaps the most important space is the Bramante cloister, which was commissioned in 1504 by Cardinal Carafa. Donato Bramante eventually worked on the grand plan for the construction of St Peter's.

Street of the Old Government

Facing away from Santa Maria della Pace, head south along the Via di Parione to the Via del Governo Vecchio (street of the old government). This lovely cobbled lane is chock-full of boutiques, vintage shops, bijou jewellery stores and clubs. The best pizzeria in Rome is located just up the street to the right. **Da Baffetto,** see ⑪③, is a must for any pizza lover.

To continue, turn left onto the Via del Governo Vecchio and head to the small triangular-shaped Piazza di Pasquino.

PIAZZA DI PASQUINO

This piazza turned car park is home to one of Rome's legendary characters,

Pasquino ❹, on a pedestal at one end of the piazza. The statue was placed on display in 1501 by Cardinal Carafa, where it quickly assumed the role of 'talking statue' *(see feature box, p.41)*. For the past five hundred years Pasquino has acted as a kind of outlet for public expression. Political satire or notes against papal policy are posted anonymously, and can still be found on the front of the plinth. Pasquino's commentary is still occasionally quoted in the daily newspapers.

CAMPO DE' FIORI

Continue south on Via di San Pantaleo and cross the busy Corso Vittorio Emanuele II *(see margin, p.40)* onto the Piazza della Cancelleria (Papal Chancellery). Just off this street is another excellent restaurant option at **Ditirambo**, see ⑪④.

The Piazza's History

Just past the Palazzo della Cancelleria is the piazza of the **Campo de' Fiori ❺** (Field of Flowers). The 'campo' has really been the centre of Roman life since at least the 15th century. At one point is was a simple flower field, but over the years it has been a meat market, a site for public execution and political rallies, a fruit and flower market, and home to numerous bars and restaurants. It can be said that this is the only true square in the city, in that it is the one piazza not attached to a temple or church.

During the medieval period the piazza was the main market and focal point for the influx of pilgrims. Many of the street names in the surrounding area still reflect their medieval use. Via dei Balestrari was where crossbow makers worked, Via dei Cappellari was for hat-makers and Via dei Chiavari was dedicated to locksmiths. The current look of the piazza is related to urban planning in the 15th century after the return of the papacy from France, an event that dramatically changed the city. In the middle of the piazza is a statue commemorating the philosopher Giordano Bruno, who was burnt at the stake in Campo de' Fiori in 1600. Bruno was found guilty of heresy for believing that the earth was

Above from far left: parade of priests; flowers for sale on the Campo de' Fiori; local mutt.

Food and Drink

① OSTERIA DEL ANIMA
Via Santa Maria dell'Anima 8; tel: 06-686 4661; noon–11.30pm; €€
This osteria has both indoor and outdoor seating and an extensive menu. Their signature pear-filled *fiocchetti* pasta in a carrot cream is a wonderful choice, as are their fish dishes.

② ANTICO CAFFÈ DELLA PACE
Via della Pace 3; tel: 06-686 1216; Tue–Sat 9am–2.30am; €
Antiques, dark wood and a lovely copper espresso machine set the tone for the interior here. Outdoor tables are on a picturesque corner. Perfect for an aperitif or a nibble.

③ DA BAFFETTO
Via del Governo Vecchio 114; tel: 06-686 1617; 6pm–1am; €
Stop in for a legendary thin-crust pizza. Baffetto is only open in the evenings and gets packed out, so be prepared to wait in the queue for a table. Not elegant, but definitely excellent.

④ DITIRAMBO
Piazza della Cancelleria 74; tel: 06-687 1626; Mon 7.30–11.30pm, Tue–Sat 1–3pm, 7.30–11.30pm; €€
This is a failsafe choice for an excellent dinner (largely organic), at a fair price, in a good location. They have typical seasonal dishes like bean soup, as well as specialities like ravioli with pumpkin sauce. There are very few tables so book ahead.

'Modern' Boulevard

Corso Vittorio Emanuele II was part of the massive renovation plan that changed the face of Rome after the Unification in the 1870s. The street was put in to create a 'modern' boulevard that would conduct the flow of traffic between key points across the city. It was successful in that it is one of the largest and most congested roads. Sadly, the construction of this smog-filled street separated the once intertwined neighbourhoods around Piazza Navona and Campo de' Fiori. In order to create a straight road many of the characteristic medieval houses were torn down.

not the centre of the universe. The philosopher was the originator of the concept of 'free thought'.

The Piazza Today

Today the busy Campo de' Fiori continues to be a hub of sorts. A wonderful fruit and vegetable market still sets up each morning at dawn (Mon–Sat). By lunchtime, when the market closes for the day, groups of local businessmen and women can be seen eating on the square. In the evenings strolling families fill the piazza, and by nightfall the restaurants and bars are crammed with university students.

The Neighbourhood

Taking the Via dei Capellari, from the west side of the piazza, leads you into the surrounding medieval quarter. Continue to the Via del Pellegrino (the pilgrims' way), which, as the name suggests, was constructed to deal with the flow of traffic for pilgrims visiting St Peter's. Keeping left brings you to a small piazza. Make a sharp left turn onto the Via Monserrato, the more elegant of the medieval streets.

Nearby, on the Via dei Banchi Vecchi is **Il Goccetto**, see ⑪⑤, a charming little wine bar.

Continue east on Via Monserrato to the lovely Piazza Farnese. Though the space actually adjoins the Campo de' Fiori this piazza feels worlds apart.

PIAZZA FARNESE

The focal point of the **Piazza Farnese** ❻ is the **Palazzo Farnese** (closed to the public), considered the finest of the Renaissance palaces. The palazzo was begun for Pope Paul III while he was still Cardinal Farnese. Work started in 1514 by Antonio da Sangallo, and was passed along to Michelangelo who added the upper floors and the finely ordered decoration. The two massive basins in the piazza were taken from the Baths of Caracalla *(see p.33)*. Palazzo Farnese is now home to the French Embassy.

PALAZZO SPADA

One street off the Piazza Farnese, on the Via Capo di Ferro, sits the small **Palazzo Spada** ❼ (Piazza Capo di Ferro 13; tel: 06-32810; www.galleria borghese.it; Tue–Sun 8.30am–7.30pm; charge). This ingenious palazzo is recognizable by its stuccoed facade of the 1540s. Borromini was commissioned to modify the space, and he added a *trompe l'oeil* (fool the eye) masterpiece of false perspective. In order to create the look of a non-existent garden, he constructed a tiny colonnade that creates the perception of a large garden

---

Below: Palazzo Spada garden.

Food and Drink 🍴

⑤ IL GOCCETTO

Via dei Banchi Vecchi 14; €

This traditional pre-dinner wine bar serves some fantastic wines by the glass. The feeling is relaxed yet they have over 800 wines on hand for purchase. Don't be afraid to ask questions. The cheese plates or salmon rolls are a perfect addition to any bottle.

portico. Part of the palace now houses offices of the High Court, and the public galleries display Cardinal Spada's exceptional art collection. Exhibits are unmarked works by Titian, Guercino, Rubens, Caravaggio, Domenichino, Parmigianino, as well as Andrea del Sarto, and both Orazio and Artemisia Gentileschi.

THEATRE OF POMPEY

Take the Via dei Balestrari to the edge of the Campo de' Fiori, and turn right, heading east into the pedestrian shopping street of Via dei Giubbonari. Turn left on Via dei Chiavari; at the first left is a small street with tall buildings following the curve of the **Teatro di Pompeo** ❽ (Theatre of Pompey). The original theatre was built in 55 BC, and was not only the world's largest theatre but also the first permanent one. It was here, in the attached Curia Pompeia, that Julius Caesar was stabbed to death in 44 BC.

SANT'ANDREA DELLA VALLE

At the end of the street, facing the traffic of the Corso Vittorio Emanuele II, is the church of **Sant'Andrea della Valle** ❾ (Piazza Sant'Andrea della Valle, tel: 06-686 1339; 7.30am–12.30pm, 4.30–7.30pm; free). This large structure sits directly on the busy Corso, making it difficult to appreciate the size of the church and dome. Construction was carried out in two phases and completed by Carlo

Maderno in 1625. The massive dome and windows make this one of the best naturally lit churches in the city. The interior decoration is in keeping with the high Baroque style, and the swirling ceiling frescoes depicting the *Glory of Paradise* by Giovanni Lanfranco are a prime example of the tastes of the period. There are often summer and evening concerts performed at this centrally located church. Check postings at the entrance for the concert schedule.

Above from far left: one of Piazza Farnese's basins; Palazzo Spada's facade; cafés on Piazza Farnese.

The Talking Statues

There are a total of six 'talking statues' in the city, collectively known as Il Congresso degli Arguti (the Congress of the Shrewd). The statues formed a sort of anonymous political forum in 15th-century Rome, at a time when papal censorship was strictly enforced. Criticism was originally directed towards political injustices and corruption in the Church, but eventually included lampooning. This anonymous commentary generally took the form of poems written in local dialect (the language of the people). While Pasquino was undoubtedly the first statue to start the tradition the other four soon followed suit. They were set up at various points around the city and often maintained an ongoing written dialogue with each other based in ironic retort. The other 'talking statues' are Marforio, Facchino, Abate Luigi, Madama Lucrezia and Babuino. Pasquino is the only one still in use (*right*).

4

ARA PACIS TO THE PANTHEON

Tucked away in a relatively small area of the centre are some of the most inspiring monuments in Rome. This route covers the emblematic Ara Pacis, the elegance of the Galleria Pamphilj and the wonder of the Pantheon.

Keeping Peace
The new Ara Pacis building is full of natural light and unobtrusive clean lines, but it has provoked strong reactions from Romans. It's the first modern building to be constructed in the historic centre since Mussolini's Fascist era, and is a little too modern for some tastes. The vast sums spent on the project are difficult to justify, say its detractors, in a city with thousands of neglected archae-ological remains.

DISTANCE 2km (1¼ miles)
TIME A half day
START Ara Pacis
END Piazza della Rotonda
POINTS TO NOTE

This is a great walk for morning or afternoon. There is a lot to take in but the route is contained in a fairly small geographical area. Note that the Galleria Doria Pamphilj has an early closing time of 5pm. Children generally like this route.

Start on the Via di Ripetta, just south of the Piazza del Popolo or a few minutes stroll west of the Spanish Steps.

ARA PACIS

The **Museo dell'Ara Pacis ❶** (Ara Pacis Museum; Piazza Augusto Imperatore, tel: 06-8205 9127; www.arapacis.it; Tue–Sun 9am–7pm; charge) is a dazzling white structure designed by Richard Meier to house the Ara Pacis Augustae (Altar of Majestic Peace), one of the best examples of early Roman sculpture. The dramatic looking building has provoked strong controversy in Rome *(see margin, left)*.

The focal point of the museum is the grand altar; what we see today are the remaining sections of a large sacrificial altar used for public ceremony and offerings of peace. The altar was consecrated in 9 BC under the Emperor Augustus to celebrate his war victories in Gaul and Hispania, and became the most important symbol of the Pax Romana, a time of peace and prosperity from 27 BC to 180 AD. The beautiful and unusually life-like relief carvings depict Augustus and his family in the sacrificial processional of 13 BC.

MAUSOLEUM OF AUGUSTUS

Next to the Ara Pacis is the overgrown **Mausoleo di Augusto ❷**, located in the piazza. This now dilapidated ruin would have been finished with carved marble decorations and statuary. The circular building was built in 28 BC as a family mausoleum, and the funerary urns of the Emperors Tiberius, Caligula and Claudius were also placed here. The entrance was marked with Egyptian obelisks, which now stand in the Piazza del Quirinale *(see p.50)* and at Santa Maria Maggiore *(see p.79)*.

On two sides of the piazza is a

Fascist-era colonnade, home to some great eateries. Try **Gusto**, see ⑪①, where the outdoor seating extends under the covered portico.

Ice Cream and Refreshments

Exit the Piazza Augusto Imperatore at the southwest corner, where Via di Ripetta becomes Via della Scrofa. At no. 104 is the ever-popular **Alfredo's**, see ⑪②, which claims to have invented the deliciously calorific Alfredo sauce. Off the Via della Scrofa, east along the Via della Stel-

letta, which becomes Via degli Ufficio del Vicario, you will see **Giolitti**, see ⑪③ (at no. 40), home to the best gelato in the city. They have been perfecting their family recipe since 1870.

GOVERNMENT BUILDINGS

Continue to the nearby Piazza di Montecitorio located at the end of the street. The square is named after the fortress-like **Palazzo di Montecitorio** ❸, designed by Gianlorenzo Bernini in the 1620s; today it is the seat of the

Above from far left: Ara Pacis; home to Rome's best ice cream; Mausoleum of Augustus.

Below: choose your favourite at Giolitti.

Food and Drink ⑪

① GUSTO
Piazza Augusto Imperatore; tel: 06-322 6273; noon–11pm; €€–€€€ or €–€€
The pizzeria and the outdoor café and bar are the most economical options, while the osteria and restaurant are pricier, but offer an extended menu to match. The food is generally traditional Roman dishes mixed with modern fusion.

② ALFREDO ALLA SCROFA
Via della Scrofa 104; tel: 06-6880 6163; 12.30–3pm, 6–11.30pm; €€€
The traditional Roman feel and great food (like the fettuccine Alfredo) keep this place popular. Other specialities include pasta al Gorgonzola and anything with a white truffle sauce.

③ GIOLITTI
Via degli Ufficio del Vicario 40; tel: 06-699 1243; Mon–Sat 7am–1am; €
This famous gelateria serves wonderful handmade ice cream; flavours include cinnamon, and watermelon with chocolate seeds. They also serve coffee, cakes and sandwiches. Eat in or take away.

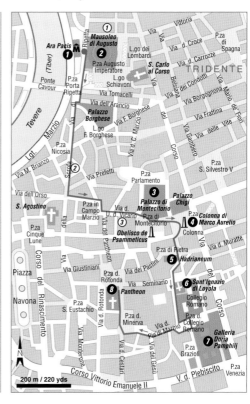

Little Chick

Gianlorenzo Bernini's statue of a playful baby elephant dates from 1667. The inspiration came from a 15th-century novel in which the protagonist meets a stone elephant carrying an obelisk. Bernini's obelisk is one of two brought to Rome by the Emperor Diocletian. The statue is often referred to as Pulcino, which is an endearing term in Roman dialect meaning 'little chick'.

Italian Chamber of Deputies (Houses of Parliament). In front sits an Egyptian obelisk dating from the 10th century BC, known as the **obelisco de Psammeticus** which comes from Heliopolis and was brought to Rome under the Emperor Augustus; its shadow indicated the time on the sundial at the Ara Pacis.

Piazza Colonna

At the far side the piazza opens onto the front of the adjoining **Palazzo Chigi**, housing the office of the prime minister. The open square in front of the palazzo is known as the **Piazza Colonna**, after the **Colonna di Marco Aurelio** ❹ (column of Marcus Aurelius) that stands in the centre.

This 30-m (100-ft) high column is a triumphal monument depicting the war victories of the Emperor Marcus Aure-

Right: Egyptian obelisk in front of Palazzo di Montecitorio.

lius in 176 AD. It is made in the style of Trajan's Column *(see p.29)*, and carved out of 28 fitted blocks of Carrara marble. The relief carving flows in a continual spiral from the ground upwards, revealing all of the battle details in chronological order.

Just south of the Piazza Colonna is the tidy Piazza di Pietra with remnants of the **Hadrianeum** ❺ (Temple of Hadrian). All that remains of the second-century temple are the eleven fluted Corinthian columns, encased in what is now part of the stock exchange.

SANT' IGNAZIO DI LOYOLA

Continuing south along the tiny Via de' Burro is the Baroque wonder of **Sant'Ignazio di Loyola** ❻ (Piazza di Sant'Ignazio; tel: 06-679 4406; www.chiesasantignazio.org; 7.30am–noon, 3–7pm; free). It was built under the patronage of Cardinal Ludovesi in 1626, and is most famous for its Baroque interior and masterpieces of decorative illusion. The nave ceiling is covered with the bright frescoes by Andrea Pozzo, who used the *trompe l'oeil* (fool the eye) technique to create three-dimensional space. Further along the nave is a spot on the floor marking the ideal vantage point to see the dome. Look carefully as this is also a trick of the artist. The dome is false, having been painted on a flat surface.

At the back of the church, along the Via Sant'Ignazio, is the parking area of the Piazza del Collegio Romano and the entrance to the Galleria Doria

Pamphilj. The palace is still inhabited by the Pamphilj family who own one of the best private art collections in Italy.

GALLERIA DORIA PAMPHILJ

Entering the **Galleria Doria Pamphilj** ❼ (Piazza del Collegio Romano 2 or Via del Corso 305; tel: 06-679 7323; www.doriapamphilj.it; Fri–Wed 10am–5pm; charge) is like stepping back in time to the 17th century. The art collection was started by Pope Innocent X Pamphilj, and now includes over four hundred paintings. Highlights include art by Titian, Raphael, Brueghel, Ribera, Correggio and Parmigianino. Of note are rare early works by Caravaggio, such as the *Repentant Magdalen*, and the powerful *Portrait of Pope Innocent X* by Velázquez displayed next to the *Bust of Pope Innocent X* by Bernini.

THE PANTHEON

Continue the route at the Piazza del Collegio Romano walking west along the Via del Pie' di Marmo to the Piazza della Minerva, with the elephant statue *(see margin, left)* and around to the front of the Pantheon.

The **Pantheon** ❽, also known as the Basilica di Santa Maria ad Martyres (Piazza della Rotonda; tel: 06-6830 0230; Mon–Sat 8.30am–7.30pm, Sun 9am–6pm; free), is one of the most complex and beautifully designed buildings in the world. The present structure has been in continuous use since it was built in 125 AD under the Emperor Hadrian. It was designed as a temple to the 12 most important classical gods with the functional space reinforcing the concept. In 608, under the Emperor Phocas, the Pantheon was converted from a pagan temple to the church of St Mary of the Martyrs. This act likely saved it from complete destruction.

Interior

The impact of walking through the original bronze doors into the Pantheon is staggering. The height and diameter of the coffered dome are exactly the same measurement (43.3m/142ft), meaning that the space inside creates a perfect sphere, the symbol of spiritual perfection. Light enters through the open oculus above, a circular hole measuring 9m (30ft) in diameter, symbolically linking the temple and the heavens on high. The coffered part of the dome was constructed out of poured concrete that progressively thins near the top edge. The walls are 6m (20ft) thick at their base to support the weight of the massive structure. Much of the interior marble decoration and flooring is original, but there have been additions and modifications. The tomb of Raphael can be found to the left of the main altar, opposite that of King Vittorio Emanuele I.

Piazza della Rotonda

The Piazza della Rotonda at the front of the Pantheon has been written about, painted and photographed for generations. In the centre is a fountain with steps supporting a small but elegant obelisk from the Temple of Isis.

Above from far left: Bernini's elephant statue on Piazza della Minerva; facade on Piazza Navona; crowds outside the Pantheon.

Below: detail from the Pantheon facade; the oculus.

SPANISH STEPS, TRIDENT AND TREVI FOUNTAIN

This walk covers Rome's fashionable shopping district. The grand Spanish Steps give way to the Via dei Condotti, one of the most exclusive and understated retail addresses in the world; and not far away is the delightful Trevi Fountain.

DISTANCE 2.5km (1½ miles)

TIME A half day

START Piazza di Spagna

END Trevi Fountain

POINTS TO NOTE

There are plenty of opportunities to stop and relax, people-watch or window shop along this route. The area is full of attractive cafés. Consider either starting quite early in the morning, or in the cool of the late afternoon. Many of the shops stay open in the summer until 8pm.

The walk begins at the Piazza di Spagna (metro line A, Spagna), a lively space that could be called the city centre. The piazza has been Rome's most popular meeting point for centuries.

PIAZZA DI SPAGNA

At the centre of the **Piazza di Spagna** ❶ is the early Baroque fountain called **Fontana della Barcaccia** (Fountain of the Ugly Boat). The basin looks like an ancient sailing vessel and was designed in 1625 by Pietro Bernini, father to the more famous Gian Lorenzo. It has sup-

plied clean drinking water and a focal point to the piazza for generations. Leading away from the piazza is the elegant, and expensive, Via dei Condotti, with shops such as Yves St Laurent and Christian Dior cornering the square.

Spanish Steps

Straight up from the piazza are the picture-perfect **scalinata di Trinità dei Monti** or **Spanish Steps** ❷. On the right corner as you look up is the house where John Keats lived until his death in 1821. His friend Percy Shelley wrote the poem *Mourn not for Adonis* in honour of the sombre occasion. Shelley drowned the following year off the coast of La Spezia. Both writers are buried in Rome's Protestant Cemetery *(see p.75)*, and the house on the Spanish Steps has been turned into the **Keats-Shelley Memorial House** ❸ (Piazza di Spagna 26; tel: 06-678 4235; www.keats-shelley-house.org; Mon–Fri 9am–1pm, 3–6pm, Sat 11am–2pm; charge). The small museum displays a collection of memorabilia.

On the opposite side, to the left of the steps, are the legendary tearooms at **Babington's**, see ⑪①. They have been serving English travellers since 1896.

Stepping Lightly

The funding for the Spanish Steps (built in 1725) came through the French diplomat Etienne Gueffier; he proposed covering the muddy slope between the French church of the Trinità dei Monti and the Palazzo Monaldeschi in the piazza below. Unfortunately for the patrons, the palazzo was home to the Spanish Embassy to the Holy See, who were not in favour of a royal monument dominating their papal city. Though the steps were conceived and paid for by French diplomats, and they lead up to the French church and French Academy, they are still known as the Spanish Steps.

Trinità dei Monti

At the top of the 137 steps is the crowning terrace and the Egyptian obelisk found in the Gardens of Sallust. Above is the elegant facade of the church of **Trinità dei Monti** (Piazza Trinità dei Monti; tel: 06-679 4179; 9am–1pm, 3–7pm; free), with matching bell-towers creating the architectural symmetry. The church was constructed in 1502 under the patronage of the French King Louis XII. Inside is a colourful fresco series by Taddeo Zuccari and two paintings by Daniele da Volterra, Michelangelo's student and assistant.

Villa Medici

To the left of the church, along the Viale Trinità dei Monti, is the Tuscan inspired **Villa Medici** that now houses the **Accademia di Francia** (French Academy; tel: 06-67611; www.villa medici.it; open for exhibitions and concerts, or by appointment). The villa was once owned by Cardinal Ferdinando I de' Medici, Grand Duke of Tuscany, who amassed a great art collection to rival that of the Borghese nearby. The building was later taken over by the French Academy, which was founded in 1666 by Louis XIV for the education of painters in Rome.

Both Poussin and Ingres were directors, and famous students included Fragonard, Boucher and Debussy. The handsome **Villa Medici gardens** (Sat and Sun 10.30–11.30am; free) were once described by Henry James as 'the most enchanting' place in Rome.

TRIDENT

Return to Piazza di Spagna, and head north along the Via del Babuino, turn right onto Via degli Orti d'Alibert, and left onto the Via Margutta. This hidden street still exudes the charm of the 1960s cinema world, made famous by directors like Federico Fellini. Via Margutta is a

Above from far left: Spanish Steps overlooked by the church of Trinità dei Monti; shopping by the steps.

Food and Drink

① **BABINGTON'S TEA ROOMS**
Piazza di Spagna 23; tel: 06-678 6027; www.babingtons.net; Mon–Wed 9am–8pm; €–€
These pleasant tearooms have an old world charm. Perfect for afternoon tea, but also suitable for a light lunch or a bacon and egg breakfast. Not inexpensive but the quality is excellent.

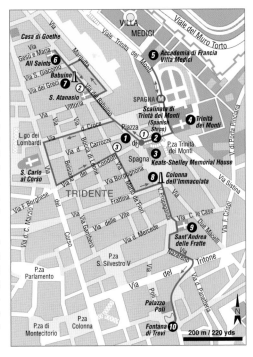

Baboon Face

The statue of Babuino is a fairly unattractive reclining figure sitting at a fountain basin. The body depicts a woodland satyr from Greek mythology, while the head is from another figure. The effect of these two incongruous parts gave rise to the Renaissance nickname 'baboon face' or Babuino. He is so much a part of the Roman landscape that he has a street named after him.

sort of Roman Hollywood. Browse the interesting shops and galleries, and turn left at the Via del Orto di Napoli to rejoin the Via del Babuino.

Via del Babuino

To the right of the intersection is the Anglican church of **All Saints** ⑥ (Via del Babuino 153; tel: 06-3600 1881; www.allsaintsrome.org; Mon–Fri 8am–7pm, Sun services; free) constructed in Victorian brickwork.

The **Via del Babuino** is one of the three major shopping streets that make up the area called the 'Trident'. The other two are Via del Corso and Via di Ripetta, and they all radiate out from the Piazza del Popolo like prongs of a fork. The three main streets and smaller connecting lanes create an intriguing area that has subtle elegance. The Via del Babuino was once home to artists' studios and workshops, and now accommodates antique dealers and designers. Walking along the street back towards the Spanish

Steps you will see the reclining statue of **Babuino** ⑦, who lends his name to the street *(see margin, left)*. Between the statue and the Greek national church of Sant'Atanasio is the artist's studio that once belonged to neoclassical sculptor Antonio Canova and his assistant Adamo Tadolini. The space is now an interesting café-museum. The **Café Atelier Canova-Tadolini**, see ⑪② (Via del Babuino 150; tel: 06-3211 0702; www.museoateliercanovatadolini.it; Mon–Sat 8am–8.30pm; free), serves excellent coffee and snacks at tables nestled between the artist's tools and plaster studio models. It is worth a look inside just to see the artwork.

Via del Corso

Turn right at the Via della Croce into the smaller shopping streets between the Trident. Turn left at the **Via del Corso**, the longest and straightest of the roads, and considered the city's only high-street shopping district.

Via dei Condotti

Turn left again onto the **Via dei Condotti** (now facing the full view of the Spanish Steps at the end of the street). Window-shopping is appropriate, unless you feel like browsing for the latest look at Giorgio Armani or admiring hand-constructed jewellery at the prestigious Buccellati. Just past the Via Mario de' Fiori is the coffee house of coffee houses – the **Antico Caffè Greco**, see ⑪③. This café has been serving the world's intellectuals since 1760. Customers such as Keats, Goethe, Liszt, Casanova, Buffalo Bill,

---

Food and Drink 🍴

② CAFÉ ATELIER CANOVA-TADOLINI
Via del Babuino 150; tel: 06-3211 0702; Mon–Sat 8am–8.30pm; €–€€
Hunger is a good excuse to come in and look around this lovely museum with a café attached. They serve excellent cappuccino at the bar, or more substantial pastas, salads and seasonal dishes at the tables.

③ ANTICO CAFFÈ GRECO
Via dei Condotti 86; tel: 06-6791 700; Mon–Sat 9am–7.30pm; €
Most of the lovely tables in the back room are packed with international tourists. It is hard to fault people for wanting to stop here. Try ordering a coffee and a cake standing at the bar for a less expensive option.

and King Ludwig have found comfort in the velvet sofas and intimate salons.

Colonna dell'Immacolata

From the Caffè Greco, retrace your steps, turning south along the Via Mario de' Fiori, and turn left at Via Frattina. In the piazza at the corner of the Via Propaganda is the **Colonna dell'Immacolata ❽**, a large column topped by a statue of the Virgin Mary. The monument is dedicated to the Immaculate Conception, as part of the church dogma agreed upon under Pope Pius IX. The erection of the column in 1857 required the assistance of 220 members of the Fire Brigade, who now consider this monument their protector.

Sant'Andrea delle Fratte

Take the Via Propaganda to the church of **Sant'Andrea delle Fratte ❾** (Piazza Sant'Andrea delle Fratte 1; tel: 06-679 3191; 7.30am–12.30pm, 4–7pm; free) one of the great remodelling efforts of Francesco Borromini

from the 1670s. The dome frescoes by Pasquale Marini, and oversized angel statues by Gianlorenzo Bernini are particularly lovely.

TREVI FOUNTAIN

Continue along, crossing over the busy Via del Tritone, and onto the Via della Stamperia. The sound of water is audible before the **Fontana di Trevi ❿** comes into view. This immense, and popular, fountain is always crowded.

The Trevi Fountain was completed in 1762, making it a relative newcomer to the urban landscape. The theme celebrates the flow of fresh water into the city, and the name Trevi *(tre vie)* alludes to the juncture of three 'roads' of water, this being the meeting of the Aqua Vergine, the Aqua Virgo and one of the repaired ancient aqueducts. Depicted is the muscular Neptune on a shell chariot *(see feature box)*, who dominates the setting. The entire scene is set against the back of the Palazzo Polli.

Toss a Coin
Popular tradition holds that if you throw a coin into the Trevi Fountain, you will return to Rome. Facing away from the fountain, hold the coin in your right hand, and toss it over your left shoulder.

Sea God

The focus of Nicola Salvi's fountain design is the powerful sea god Neptune. Each of Neptune's Tritons have seahorse chargers, one with an unruly horse representing the oceans or stormy weather, the other with a docile horse representing lakes or still waters. The arrival of the water itself is being heralded by blasts from conch shell horns. At the sides of the main scene are allegorical statues representing health (right) and abundance (left), symbols of the properties of water. A marble relief shows Agrippa commissioning the aqueduct in 19BC. Salvi incorporated numerous varieties of water plants in the composition.

QUIRINALE, BARBERINI AND VIA VENETO

Taking in the palaces of the President of the Republic, past Baroque monuments and the rarefied air of the Via Veneto, this walk includes some of the glamour spots of the city centre.

DISTANCE 2km (1½ miles)
TIME A half day
START Piazza del Quirinale
END Via Veneto at Porta Pinciana
POINTS TO NOTE

If you follow this route in the morning, you could stop for lunch at the top of the Via Veneto, and continue to walk 7 for a full-day itinerary. Note that the Quirinal Palace is only open to the public on Sunday mornings.

Bee for Barberini

The Barberini are considered one of the most influential and powerful families in the history of Rome. They first arrived in the late 16th century form Florence, where they went by the name of Tafani, meaning 'horsefly'. The family emblem was this rather unattractive insect. With their pre-sentation into the new city the Tafani changed their surname to Barberini, and altered the emblem to resemble the ancient royal symbol of a bee. Barberini bees can still be found on a number of outdoor monuments and palazzi throughout the city.

Food and Drink 🍽️

① CAFFETTERIA SCUDERIE DEL QUIRINALE

Via XXIV Maggio (inside the museum); tel: 06-6962 7221; opening times follow exhibition schedule; €

This is an excellent museum café offering pastries, tea, coffee, lunch and hot-bar selection. The bright tables have views onto the piazza and the city below.

This route begins at the stately piazza in front of the Palazzo del Quirinale, located a few minutes south of the Trevi Fountain, and just up from the Via Nazionale.

QUIRINALE

The panoramic **Piazza del Quirinale** is the grand entrance to the **Palazzo del Quirinale ❶** (Quirinal Palace; tel: 06-46991; www.quirinale.it; Sun 8.30am–noon; charge). This secured complex was originally built over the ruins of the Baths of Constantine. The Renaissance buildings were constructed as the papal summer palaces, and were later used by the new king after Unification in the 1870s. It now serves as the official residence of the President of the Italian Republic. The focal point of the piazza is the fountain with ancient statues of the twin *Dioscuri* (horse tamers) Castor and Pollux, found in the excavation of the Baths of Constantine. The fountain is crowned by an Egyptian obelisk, which stood at the Mausoleum of Emperor Augustus and was moved to its present location in the 18th century.

Scuderie del Quirinale

At the corner of the piazza is the **Scuderie del Quirinale ❷** (Quirinale stables; Via XXIV Maggio; tel: 06-996 7500; www.scuderiequirinale.it; Sun–Thur 10am–8pm, Fri–Sat 10am–

10.30pm; charge). The stables were added in 1732 and were in active use until 1932 when motorised cars supplanted horse-drawn carriages. The Scuderie is now a museum and exhibition space. This bright gallery displays a selection of paintings from the palace, as well as a set of papal carriages.

The modern **museum café**, see ⑪①, is fine for a break. The bookstore also stocks excellent art books.

Sant'Andrea al Quirinale

Along the Via del Quirinale, past a pleasant shady park, is Gianlorenzo Bernini's grand church of **Sant' Andrea al Quirinale** ❸ (Via del Quirinale 29; tel: 06-474 4872; daily 8.30am–noon, 4pm–7pm; free), known as the 'pearl of the Baroque'. The decorative scheme of the interior works collectively to provide a harmonious dialogue between the sculpture, oval dome and inlaid marble. Though Sant'Andrea is not as grand as the piazza of St Peter's, Bernini considered it his best architectural achievement.

Four Fountains

The church is nicely contrasted with that of **San Carlo alle Quattro Fontane** ❹ (Via del Quirinale 23; tel: 06-488 3261; Mon–Fri and Sun 10am–1pm, 3–6pm, Sat 10am–1pm; free), designed in 1667 by Bernini's rival Francesco Borromini. The real measurements of the tiny building are ingeniously disguised through the use of architectural and decorative illusion. Borromini used his signature curving architecture to provide an airy feel.

At the junction is the unusual monument of **Le Quattro Fontane** (Four Fountains), mounted on the corners of the buildings facing the intersection. The allegorical figures were designed by Domenico Fontana and represent the *Tiber*, the *Arno*, *Fidelity* and *Strength*. The Baroque fountain was constructed as part of the urban redevelopment plan of the 1580s under Pope Sixtus V. The street was then called the Via Felice (street of happiness) as it connects the

Above from far left: guards outside the Palazzo del Quirinale; allegorical figure of the Arno, one of the Quattro Fontane; papal coat of arms of Sant'Andrea al Quirinale; Fontana del Tritone on Piazza Barberini.

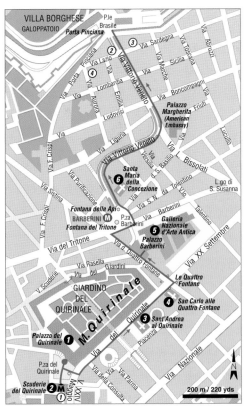

churches of Trinità dei Monti, above the Spanish Steps, with Santa Maria Maggiore. The obelisks marking each of these churches can be seen from the junction.

PALAZZO BARBERINI

Along the Via delle Quattro Fontane is the entrance to one of Rome's best art museums, located inside the **Palazzo Barberini**, now the **Galleria Nazionale d'Arte Antica** ❺ (Via Barberini 18; tel: 06-481 4591; www.galleriaborghese.it; Tue–Sun 9am–7pm; charge).

Pope Urban VIII Barberini commissioned some of the top 17th-century architects for the construction of his family palace. The sumptuous rooms and rich decoration display the tastes of one of the city's most powerful popes, and the Barberini inhabited the upper floors until the 1960s.

Highlights are a series of grand halls and Rococo apartments (closed for restoration until 2009), and a fresco series by Pietro da Cortona depicting the *Triumph of Divine Providence*, which artfully alludes to the papacy of Urban VIII by displaying his full astrological chart. Paintings in the galleries include works by El Greco, Caravaggio, Guido Reni, Tintoretto, a formal portrait of King Henry VIII by Holbein, and the seductive *La Fornarina* by Raphael *(see margin, left)*. The national art collection is divided with the Palazzo Corsini *(see p.66)*.

Piazza Barberini

In the nearby **Piazza Barberini**, at the centre of the clogged intersection where seven streets converge, you will discover the playful **Fontana del Tritone**. The leaping dolphins and muscular Triton with serpent legs were designed by Bernini in 1642 to promote the career of Urban VIII. The papal tiara, keys of St Peter, and the heraldic bee emblems of the Barberini family are integrated into the composition. Across the square is the smaller **Fontana delle Api** (Fountain of the Bees) from 1641, showcasing the family bees *(see margin, p.50)*.

VIA VENETO

At the nothern side of the piazza is the start of the Via Vittorio Veneto of *La Dolce Vita* fame. The curving tree-lined street has had its share of celebrity, but

it is now less desirable. The trendy cafés and restaurants caught by the flash of the 1960s paparazzi have been replaced with pricey brasseries, embassies and some of Rome's most luxurious hotels.

A few of the infamous haunts are still open, such as Café de Paris at no. 90 or Doney's at no. 145, but the quality of these places has reduced in proportion to their inflated prices. The best choice for lounging in a sophisticated retro atmosphere is **Harry's Bar**, see 🍴②, for drinks or a meal. Many tour groups funnel into the Hard Rock Café at no. 62 for American-style hamburgers and beers. However, a trip to Rome would not be complete without a stroll along this shady boulevard.

Santa Maria della Concezione

Just up from the Piazza Barberini is one of the Via Veneto's strangest sights, located at the church of **Santa Maria della Concezione** ⑥ (Via Vittorio Veneto 27; tel: 06-487 1185; www.capucciniviaveneto.it; church 7am–noon, 3–7pm, crypt 9am–noon, 3–6pm; donation). The lower level crypt is the place that draws the crowds, with a display of some macabre relics. Here the skeletal remains of more than 4,000 Capuchin monks are arranged in artistic patterns. If the bones themselves are not sombre enough, the sign at the entrance reads 'What you are now, we once were. What we are now, you shall someday become'.

For something lighter have a look at the paintings by Guido Reni and Pietro da Cortona in the main church.

Porta Pinciana

Continue the walk up the meandering Via Veneto, past the regal Excelsior Hotel at no. 125, and the 1890s Palazzo Margherita (now the American Embassy), to end at the **Porta Pinciana**, one of the gateways into the park of the Villa Borghese.

The Porta Pinciana is one of the ancient entries into the city through the Aurelian Walls, which were originally built in 275 under the Emperor Aurelian. The walls once enclosed all seven hills of Rome, including the left bank and the neighbourhood of Trastevere. Only a few sections remain standing.

Located just off the Via Veneto is one of Rome's traditional cafés, **Lotti**, see 🍴③, a family-run business that dates back to 1917. Another good option is **Aurora 10 da Pino**, see 🍴④.

Above from far left: facade on Via Veneto; Porta Pinciana.

St Teresa
Head east along Via Barberini; on the corner of Piazza San Bernardo and Via XX Settembre stands the church of Santa Maria della Vittoria. It contains Bernini's famous Baroque Cornaro side-chapel, which uses natural light to highlight the *Ecstasy of St Teresa*.

Food and Drink 🍴

② HARRY'S BAR
Via Vittorio Veneto 150; tel: 06-484 643; www.harrysbar.it; restaurant open Mon–Sat 12.30–3pm, 7.30pm–1am; €€
This longstanding Roman hotspot serves long drinks in the elegant bar, and intimate lunches and dinners in the richly decorated main rooms. Try their grilled meats and steaks with a local novello wine.

③ LOTTI
Via Sardegna 19; tel: 06-482 1902; Sun–Fri 7am–10.30pm; €
A classic spot for the perfect coffee, a homemade pastry, gelato or lunch. Their hot-bar serves various vegetables, meats, and homemade pasta dishes, including the wonderful artichoke lasagna. Garden seating is available in the summer.

④ AURORA 10 DA PINO
Via Aurora 10; tel: 06 474 2779; Tue–Sun noon–3pm, 7.30–11.00pm; €€€
This restaurant and wine bar offers good food and local ambiance. Delicious seafood antipasto and main dishes of grilled fish are accompanied by an extensive wine list.

VILLA BORGHESE TO PIAZZA DEL POPOLO

This walk meanders through the most loved green space in Rome, complete with views, lakes and one of the world's finest private art collections, finishing with a look at the church of Santa Maria del Popolo.

Below: park fun.

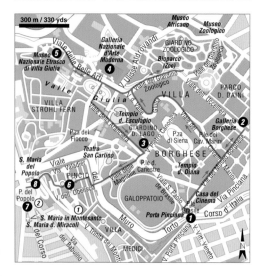

DISTANCE 3.5km (2 miles)
TIME A half day
START Porta Pinciana
END Piazza del Popolo
POINTS TO NOTE
Advanced booking is essential for the Galleria Borghese. With a morning booking consider a picnic in the park afterwards. Alternatively, do walk 6 in the morning, and book the museum for the afternoon. This is a great walk for families with children.

Start at the **Porta Pinciana ❶**, located at the top of the Via Veneto. Alternatively, the park can be reached from Metro Spagna (through the pedestrian tunnel). Taxis are the simplest option for getting to the Galleria Borghese directly.

VILLA BORGHESE

The park of the **Villa Borghese** (www.villaborghese.it) is the most popular outdoor area, and at 80ha (200 acres) the second largest park, in the city. This green space, with museums, lakes, horse track, theatres, jogging routes, tennis, temples, cycling lanes and views, was only opened as a public area in 1903.

Galleria Borghese

For nearly 300 years the villa belonged to the Borghese family who used it for entertaining and the display of their private art collection. Now considered the jewel box of Rome, the **Galleria Borghese ❷** (Piazzale Scipione Borghese 5; tel: 06-328101; www.galleriaborghese.it; Tue–Sun 9am–7pm; charge; required booking, with entry every two hours) showcases the exceptional collection of Cardinal Scipione Borghese.

The grand path of the Viale del Museo Borghese leads from the Porta

Pinciana to the front step of this 'country' villa turned museum.

The museum is arranged on two levels joined by a spiral staircase. The ground floor is home to sculpture and antiquities, with the upper floor showcasing the paintings collection. Ticketing, cloakroom, bookshop, and a small café can be found in the basement area.

History of the Collection

When Pope Paul V Borghese came into power in 1605 he quickly appointed his favourite nephew as cardinal (one of the great cases of nepotism). The young Cardinal Scipione was an avid art collector and set about purchasing properties and building a pleasure palace to house his growing collections. Scipione had an eye for combining stunning paintings, juxtaposed with classical antiquities and complemented with contemporary sculpture, most of which was commissioned for the villa itself. The collections went through two major changes with the addition of thematic ceiling decoration in the 18th century, and the loss of a large amount of artwork to the Louvre in 1809. This 'exchange' was conveniently arranged through Napoleon Bonaparte's sister, Paolina, who was married to Camillo Borghese.

Ground Floor

Do not miss the rare 4th-century floor mosaics of gladiators, surrounded by elegant sculptures of Roman gods and busts of emperors on the ground floor. Also here are three of Gianlorenzo Bernini's most famous works. These early masterpieces from the 1620s were commissioned specifically for the villa and include the brooding *David*, the sensuous *Rape of Proserpine*, and the perfect *Apollo and Daphne*, with marble leaves so thinly carved that light shines through them. Other highlights are Antonio Canova's *Venus Victrix (see margin, right)*, and five stunning paintings by Caravaggio, including the *Boy with a Basket of Fruit* and the controversial *Palafrenieri Madonna*.

Upper Floor

The upper floor, traditionally housing the living quarters, showcases two versions Bernini's official portrait bust of Cardinal Scipione (he was not happy with the first one). Also on display are some of Raphael's early works such as the brilliant altarpiece from 1507 of the *Deposition of Christ*, Correggio's evocative *Danae*, and Titian's classic *Sacred and Profane Love* from 1514.

Left: boating in the Giardino del Lago.

Above from left: conversation on Piazza del Popolo; al fresco at Café Canova; National Gallery of Modern Art; view of St Peter's from the Pincio terrace.

Forerunners
The Etruscan civilization is one of the most refined ancient cultures, and also one of the least studied. By 800 BC they were recorded as having a sophisticated government system, a unique language and religion, and an agrarian culture that relied heavily on Greek trade. They were eventually overruled and assimilated by the Roman Republic.

Borghese Park and Lake Garden

The vast gardens surrounding the villa are now home to a number of attractions. In addition to the museums there are many jogging and bicycle paths, outdoor concerts, performance, and picnic spots under the famous umbrella pines.

Walk away from the museum along Viale del Museo Borghese, turn right on Viale dei Cavalli Marini and follow the path as it becomes the winding Via di Valle Giulia. On your left is the **Giardino del Lago** ❸, with its picturesque lake and floating island temple. There is a small outdoor coffee house nearby and rowing boats for hire.

The Zoo

If you have children en route, or wish to explore some of the park's other treasures, head northeast of the lake, and at the far edge of the park is the **zoo** (Giardino Zoologico and Bioparc; tel: 06-360 8211; www.bioparc.it; Apr–Sept 9.30am–7pm, Oct–Mar 9.30am–5pm; charge).

Connected to the popular zoo and bioparc complex is the **Museo Zoologico** (Via Ulisse Aldrovandi 18; tel: 06 6710 9270; www.museodizoologia.it; Tue–Sun 9am–7pm; charge) which functions as a natural history collection with many displays.

National Gallery of Modern Art

North of the lake, at Viale delle Belle Arti 131, is the **Galleria Nazionale d'Arte Moderna** ❹ (National Gallery of Modern Art; tel: 06-3229 8451; www.gnam.beniculturali.it; Tue–Fri, Sun 8.30am–7.30pm, charge), featuring 19th- and 20th-century Italian painters. The focus is on Romantic landscapes, but there are also works by Courbet, Cezanne, Degas and Monet.

National Etruscan Museum

Continue to the far western edge of the park where there is another excellent museum housed in the **Villa Giulia**. The **Museo Nazionale Etrusco** ❺ (National Etruscan Museum; Piazzale di Villa Giulia 9; www.villaborghese.it; tel: 06-3226 5671; Tue–Sun 8.30am–7.30pm; charge) is dedicated exclusively to the collection of Etruscan artwork *(see margin, left)*. On display are some of the most important Etruscan pieces in the world. Not to be missed is the beautifully painted Faliscan-style *Crater Representing the Dawn* from the 4th century BC, an Apollo statue from the Veio site around Rome, the engraved bronze Ficorini marriage coffer, and a heartbreaking 6th-century BC sarcophagus of a married couple sharing a permanent meal into the afterlife.

Food and Drink

① CASINA VALADIER
Viale Valadier; tel: 06-6992 2090; www.casinavaladier.it; Tue–Sat 12.30–3pm, 8–11pm, Sun 12.30–3pm; €€€
The menu is not particularly memorable considering the price, but the view and the service are spectacular. It is a perfect stop for an afternoon tea or drink, or for a romantic meal.

② CAFÉ CANOVA
Piazza del Popolo 16; tel: 06-361 2231; 8am–midnight; €–€€€
The Canova has been recently remodelled and has lost some of its old world charm, but still has some of its former reputation. There is now a gift shop as well as bar and separate restaurant, with garden seating. For a snack or drink on the piazza there is the less expensive street-side café service.

The Pincio

Return to the Modern Art Museum and head south, bearing southeast past the lake until you reach Piazzale delle Canestre, where you should head southwest along Viale delle Magnolie. This leads towards the southern edge of the park and the **Giardini del Pincio** ❻ (Pincio Gardens) re-designed by Giuseppe Valadier under Napoleon in 1809. Here you will find a bicycle hire (Bici Pincio; Viale Villa Medici; daily 10am–sunset) located near the exclusive **Casina Valadier**, see ⑪①.

At the opposite side of Pincio is the **San Carlino puppet theatre** (Viale dei Bambini; tel: 06-333 5320; www.sancarlino.it; performances on Sat, Sun, closed Jan, Aug; charge) hosting traditional Italian shows for children of all ages.

The panoramic **Pincio terrace** provides stunningly romantic views, complete with St Peter's in the distance. Descend by the side stairs to the Piazza del Popolo below.

PIAZZA DEL POPOLO

The large oval **Piazza del Popolo** ❼ is the hub of the 'Trident' area, created by the fashionable streets of the Via del Babuino, Via del Corso and Via di Ripetta *(see p.47)*. The focal point of this large space is the magnificent Egyptian obelisk from 1,300 BC. It was taken from the Sun Temple in Heliopolis by the Emperor Augustus to decorate the Circus Maximus and moved to the piazza in 1589. Facing into the piazza are the twin churches of **Santa Maria dei Miracoli** and **Santa**

Maria in Montesanto, designed by Carlo Rainaldi in the 1660s.

On the corner of the piazza at Via del Babuino is the **Café Canova**, see ⑪②, a favourite spot to see or be seen at.

Santa Maria del Popolo

At the north corner of the piazza, near the **Porta Flaminia** *(see margin, right)* is the treasure-filled **Santa Maria del Popolo** ❽ (tel: 06-361 0836; Mon–Sat 7am–noon, 4–7pm, Sun 4.30–7.30pm; free). Much of the current church was constructed in 1472 under Pope Sixtus IV (best known for his commission of the Sistine Chapel). It is loaded with Renaissance masterpieces, including the Chigi chapel designed by Raphael, and Pinturicchio frescoes in the Della Rovere chapel. The finest decoration is in the Cerasi chapel where *The Crucifixion of St Peter* and the luminous *Conversion of St Paul* attest to Caravaggio's genius; each expressed with complex psychology and realism.

Roads to Rome

The Porta Flaminia (or Porta del Popolo) is one of the original gateways into the centre of Rome. Most visitors arriving at the capital city entered either from the Appian Way or from the congested Via Flaminia. The road was built in 220 AD to connect to the Adriatic coast.

Below: Santa Maria del Popolo.

THE VATICAN

The Vatican is quintessentially Roman. With over 2000 years of history, no other place embodies so much politics, history, religion and art all rolled into one relatively small space. Each century has visibly superimposed itself upon the last, forming a great historic layer cake.

DISTANCE 1.5km (1 mile), not incl. distance covered in museums
TIME A full day
START Piazza San Pietro
END Vatican Museums
POINTS TO NOTE
The Vatican can be draining with the long queues at security. Pace yourself, and bring a bottle of water. Going to the museums in the late morning or early afternoon can reduce the wait.

The start of this walk is the huge **Piazza San Pietro ❶** (St Peter's Square). There is time to look around the Basilica of St Peter's, climb the dome, and see Michelangelo's *Pietà* before walking around the fortified walls of the Vatican Museums and the Sistine Chapel.

VATICAN CITY

The Vatican is one of the most significant tourist sights in the world, with close to 40 million visitors each year. Its

Fashion Police
Appropriate clothing must be worn at all times in the Basilica of St Peter's. For both men and women this includes no shorts, no sleeveless shirts or vests, and for women no skirts above the knee. In the busy season vendors in the area sell a set of very unattractive paper trousers, at inflated prices, for those caught without acceptable attire.

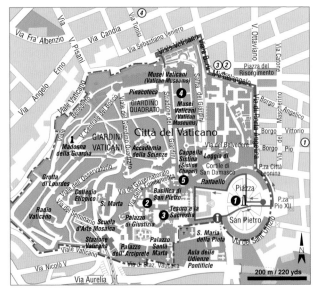

role as a political and religious power is unique, and with less than 900 inhabitants it is the world's smallest independent state. Vatican City was granted political independence from Italy in 1929, and the Pope is head of both government and state. The Vatican has its own postal system, currency, passport, licence plate, flag and police.

Vatican Hill

Vatican City sits on a large hill. The name comes from the Latin, *Mons Vaticanus* (Vatican Mount) and predates Christianity. The complex of buildings was constructed over a first-century 'circus' first built by the Emperor Caligula. The area was expanded by the Emperor Nero, who used it for games and for the persecution of Christians and other non-pagans. It was under Nero that St Peter was martyred in the circus complex. He was buried nearby on the Vatican Hill, and it was this tomb that became the centre of Christianity.

In 326 the Emperor Constantine built the first Christian temple above St Peter's tomb. This became the heart of the Catholic church, and over the centuries the area around the basilica was expanded. The original, Constantinian Basilica of St Peter's was completely torn down and built anew under the papacy of Julius II in 1506. What we now call the Vatican is primarily a Renaissance plan.

St Peter's Square

The giant elliptical-shaped piazza was added in 1656 during the final phase of decoration of the new basilica. Gianlorenzo Bernini was commissioned by Pope Alexander VII to create an architectural space that reflected the role of the church. The floor plan of the piazza is shaped like a giant keyhole, reinforcing the role of St Peter as the gatekeeper to heaven.

The focal point of the piazza is the stunning Egyptian obelisk. It was brought from the temple of Ra near Alexandria in 37 AD under the Emperor Caligula. High above Bernini's colonnade are over 200 colossal statues depicting minor saints.

Under the right colonnade is the security checkpoint to St Peter's Basilica. There is often a long queue here but it moves quite quickly. A second checkpoint near the steps is for clothing control *(see margin, left)*.

Above from far left: Giuseppe Momo's helicoidal staircase in the Vatican Museums; Piazza San Pietro.

Below: view of the keyhole-shaped square from the dome of St Peter's.

Above from left:
dome of St Peter's;
Swiss Guard; Vatican
post box; inside the
Vatican's galleries.

Papal Audiences

These are held in the Vatican on Wednesday at 10.30am, except in the height of summer, when they are at the Pope's summer residence at Castel Gandolfo outside Rome *(see p.95)*. Apply for free tickets in writing to the Prefettura della Casa Pontificia, 00120 Città del Vaticano, or go to the office on the preceding Monday or Tuesday (it's through the bronze door watched over by Swiss Guards, to the right of the basilica). For more information, tel: 06-6988 4857. The Pope comes to a window above the piazza on Sunday at noon to give the traditional angelus blessing.

ST PETER'S BASILICA

Construction of the **Basilica di San Pietro ❷** (Piazza San Pietro; tel: 06-6988 1662; www.vatican.va; 7am–7pm, until 6pm in winter; free) was a serious undertaking, with multiple architects, including Bramante, Raphael, Michelangelo (who designed the dome) and Maderno, involved. After 120 years, the building was consecrated in 1626.

The Pietà

In the right chapel, protected by thick glass, is the statue of the *Pietà* by Michelangelo. This touching depiction of the death of Christ was completed in 1499 when he was only 25.

Food and Drink 🍴

① TRE PUPAZZI
Borgo Pio 183; tel: 06-686 8371;
Tue–Sun 12.30–3.30pm, 7.30pm–
midnight; €
This excellent and inexpensive restaurant has been serving local favourites since it opened as a tavern in the 17th century. They specialise in baked dishes and veal.

② INSALATA RICCA
Piazza del Risorgimento 4; tel: 06-3973
0387; 12.30–3.30pm, 8–11pm; €€
This local chain is perfect for the Vatican location. They have a large dining area and quick service. Their huge speciality salads can even be eaten as a main dish.

③ OLD BRIDGE
Viale dei Bastioni di Michelangelo 5;
tel: 06-3972 3026; €
This tiny gelateria is full of Romans and tourists alike. The flavours are original and the portions generous.

Down the central nave, past the side chapels, is a lovely 13th-century statue of *St Peter* by Arnolfo di Cambio. This is the official representation of St Peter, and is one of the few works of art that remains from the older structure. His foot has been lovingly kissed and petted for centuries.

Works of Art

At the centre is the massive bronze *Baldacchino* hovering over the Papal altar, and marking the tomb of St Peter. This emblematic work by Bernini was commissioned by Pope Urban VIII in 1624, and is the largest freestanding bronze structure in the world *(see margin, right)*. It is dwarfed under Michelangelo's stunning cupola (dome). Just beyond the altar are more works by Bernini, the *Throne of St Peter in Glory* and window of the *Holy Spirit*. Past the apse, along the left side over a door, is the sombre monument to Pope Alexander VII. This late work by Bernini shows a bronze skeleton as the allegory of death, holding an empty hourglass.

Treasury, Grottoes and Cupola

There are separate entrances for the additional sites within St Peter's. Entrances to the **Tesoro e Sacrestia ❸** (Treasury and Sacristy; 9am–6.15pm; charge) are found on the left-hand wall of the nave; the lower level **grottoes** (7am–6pm; free) are situated on the right-hand side of the basilica, accessed from the front portico.

Another rewarding walk is the climb up to the **cupola** (8am–5.45pm; charge). Look for the entrance as it is

often rerouted for crowd control. There is a lift part way, and then another 320 steps to the top of the spectacular lantern at the top of the dome.

Lunch Stop

A break is recommended before continuing to the Vatican Museums, which are located about a 15-minute walk around the outside the Vatican walls. Just a few streets off the Via Porta Angelica the dining options become slightly more tolerable and less of an obvious tourist trap.

If time is short the **Vatican Museums Café** is an option, or you could try **Tre Pupazzi** on the Borgo Pio, see ⑪①. **Insalata Ricca**, see ⑪②, is good for fast service, and along the walls is the gelateria **Old Bridge**, see ⑪③.

VATICAN MUSEUMS

Continue along the walls to the entrance of the **Musei Vaticani** ❹ (Viale Vaticano 100; tel: 06-6988 4947; www.vatican.va; Mon–Sat 8.30am–4.00pm, closed Sun except last Sun of month, see website for other exceptions; charge; free last Sun of month). At the entry is another security checkpoint, and ticketing is located on the first floor. Maps with suggested routes are available at the entrance desk to help navigate the nearly 30 separate collections housed within 1,400 rooms. It is so vast that it is impossible to see all of the sections in one visit, so choose your favourite route. All of the itineraries take visitors through the Sistine Chapel.

Museum History

The idea of the papal collection dates to the early 1500s with Pope Julius II, who started by adding classical statuary to the courtyard of the Belvedere Palace. In the same years he commissioned Raphael to redecorate his private apartments, Bramante to start construction of the new St Peter's, and Michelangelo to decorate the ceiling of the Sistine Chapel, setting a precedence for future popes. The Vatican Museums as such were opened to the public in the 18th century.

Pinacoteca

On entering there is a choice of directions to follow. To the right, past the terrace, is the chronologically arranged

Barbarian Barberini

Bernini's elegant twisting canopy stands eight storeys tall and is solid cast in bronze. Huge amounts of resources were needed for the project, and when the metal ran out Pope Urban VIII Barberini ordered that the bronze from the portico of the Pantheon be used to complete it. This led to the pasquinade 'what the barbarians didn't do, the Barberini did'.

Below: St Peter's.

Pinacoteca (Picture Gallery). Of note is the *Stefaneschi Triptych* dating from 1298 by Giotto (better known for his frescoes in Florence). The altarpiece was commissioned for the main altar of the old Constantinian Basilica of St Peter's. Further along are some lovely fresco fragments by Melozzo da Forli, followed by three stunning altarpieces by Raphael. In the end room are two early works *The Coronation of the Virgin* and the *Madonna of Foligno* of 1511, contrasted with the massive central panel of *The Transfiguration* of 1520. This was his last project and it clearly shows the influence of Michelangelo.

Successive rooms display an unfinished Leonardo da Vinci, some lovely Titians, and large paintings on canvas form the 1600s. Particularly interesting are Guido Reni's *Crucifixion of St Peter*, and Caravaggio's unconventional *Entombment*.

Cortile della Pigna and Chiaramonti Museum

Leaving the Pinacoteca, retrace your steps to the central **Cortile della Pigna** (Pinecone Court). This open courtyard is named after the colossal bronze pinecone, displayed in a niche. The grand scale of the new St Peter's dwarfed even this massive drinking fountain, and it was moved to its present location in 1608 *(see margin, left)*.

At the far edge is the corridor of the **Museo Chiaramonti**. The static display, with original numbering system, was first laid out by Antonio Canova and shows a jumble of statues of emperors, gods, portrait busts, urns, sarcophagi and altars. The stair at the left leads into both the Egyptian Museum and the magnificent Belvedere Court.

Pio-Clementine Museum

The Belvedere Court and the Rotunda (round room) house some of the most famous classical sculptures in the world. This is the nucleus of Julius II's collections.

Both the exquisitely proportioned *Apollo Belvedere*, and the dynamic *Laocoön*, are showcased in side niches of the Octagonal Court. Further along is the Hellenistic *Belvedere Torso*. This great chunk of broken marble is still one of the most famous sculptures ever carved. At the centre of the Rotunda is a massive porphyry basin from the Emperor Nero's house.

The Corridors

Following the stairs and the flow of traffic takes you through a series of decorated corridors. The **Gallery of the Candelabra** is full of ancient Roman sculpture, which connects to the darkened **Gallery of the Tapestries**. The tapestries at the left side were made under the Flemish master weaver, Pieter Van Aelst, from incredible full-scale cartoons sent from Raphael's studio.

Through the doors is the lengthy **Corridor of Maps** commissioned by Pope Gregory XIII in 1580, and based on the work of cartographer Ignazio Danti. The route continues through several decorative rooms that lead into the apartments of Julius II.

Symbol of Unity
The great pinecone dates from the first century, and was used as a fountain in the military training grounds of the Campus Martius. Water originally flowed from the tips of each of the leaves and it was thought to be a symbol of unity. During the 8th century the fountain was moved to the courtyard of St Peter's to provide water for the visiting pilgrims.

Raphael Rooms

This series of rooms was remodelled by Raphael for the private use of Pope Julius II. They include the *Room of Constantine* and the *Expulsion of Heliodorius from the Temple*. The real masterpiece is the reading room, called the **Stanza dell Segnatura** (Room of the Signature). Raphael's frescoes carry out a philosophical dialogue across the space. On one side is the *Disputation of the Holy Sacrament*, depicting a philosophical discussion of the spiritual truths. This is juxtaposed with the *School of Athens*, a discussion of the tangible and intangible nature of philosophy.

Sistine Chapel

More is probably written about the decoration of the **Capella Sistina** ❺ than any other building in the world. The fortress-like chapel was started in 1475 under Pope Sixtus IV della Rovere, and great Renaissance painters, including Sandro Botticelli, Domenico Ghirlandaio and Pietro Perugino, executed the first phase of decoration. These frescoes illustrate scenes from the *Life of Moses* and *Life of Christ*. The ceiling decoration was commissioned in 1508 by Pope Julius II della Rovere (nephew of Sixtus IV). Michelangelo was given the task of creating a monumental image covering an area of 500 square metres (5,400 sq ft). The nine primary scenes from Genesis represent the *Separation of Light from Dark*, the *Creation of the Sun and Moon*, the *Separation of the Waters*, *Creation of Adam*, *Creation of Eve*, *Expulsion from Eden*, *Sacrifice of Noah*, the *Deluge*, and the *Drunkenness of Noah*.

Nearly 30 years later, Michelangelo was again commissioned to create the fresco on the altar wall for Pope Clement VII de Medici. The tumultuous portrayal of the *Last Judgement* has been considered both a supreme masterpiece and an affront to the church.

Library and Spiral Ramp

The exit from the Sistine Chapel generally passes by the entrance to the Vatican Library (currently closed to the public). The long corridor will bring you to the main exit, down the beautiful spiral ramp designed by Giuseppe Momo in 1932. If you are in need of a meal and a place to rest after the Vatican, the southern-style restaurant **Piacere Molise**, see ⑪④, is just a few minutes' walk north from the museum entrance.

Above from far left: the *Creation of Adam* in Michelangelo's Sistine Chapel; the Vatican Gardens.

Food and Drink 🍴

④ PIACERE MOLISE

Via Candia 60; tel: 06-3974 3553; Fri–Wed noon–3pm, 7pm–midnight; €€
A homely restaurant with a family-run feel. The menu is based on specialities of the Molise region, including spaghetti with clams and grilled fish.

Left: nun at St Peter's.

9

CASTEL SANT'ANGELO TO THE GIANICOLO

This walk showcases some of the best views and vantage points in the city. Starting with the historic and imposing Castel Sant'Angelo, down the elegant Via Giulia, to the top of the Janiculum Hill. The route includes a stop to see some of the best-kept works by Raphael.

The Executioner

The solemn role of the executioner was, as many professions in Italy, a family business. Techniques of swift execution were passed from father to son, and many learned multiple ways to get the job done. The executioner's house in medieval Rome was located between the prison of Castel Sant'Angelo and the public squares such as Campo de' Fiori. Condemned men were led across the bridge, and along the Via di Panico, to meet the executioner at his residence before continuing to the event. People would line the route in order to harangue the condemned men. Public execution was still being practised in Italy into the 19th century.

DISTANCE 3.25km (2¼ miles)
TIME A full day
START Castel Sant'Angelo
END Piazzale Giuseppe Garibaldi
POINTS TO NOTE

There is a lot to see on this route, and it is not intended that you visit every museum. Plan this route for the morning if you are considering visiting the Villa Farnesina, as it is closed in the afternoon. This route ends with a rewarding but uphill walk that includes stairs. Children usually like this walk.

CASTEL SANT'ANGELO

On the left bank near the Vatican is the **Castel Sant'Angelo ❶** (Lungotevere Castello 50; tel: 06-681 9111; www.castelsantangelo.com; Tue–Sun 9am–7pm; charge), an imposing circular brick structure that can easily be seen from central Rome. The building dates from 138 when it served as the grand-scale mausoleum for the Emperor Hadrian and his family. The mausoleum was converted into a fortress during the early 5th century, and was later given the

name Castel Sant'Angelo by Pope Gregory the Great in 590. It has since been used as a prison, and papal hideout during times of siege. A *passetto* (hidden corridor) was added in the 1270s allowing for safe passage between St Peter's and chambers inside the Castello. The 16th-century philosopher Giordano Bruno *(see p.39)* spent the last six years of his life imprisoned in the Castel Sant'Angelo before being publicly executed, see margin, for heresy in the Campo de' Fiori.

Highlights

The museum of the Castel Sant' Angelo now displays artefacts from multiple periods of Roman history. The papal chambers and the mausoleum are reached by the ancient ramp that survives from the original structure. Look for the Renaissance, hand-operated, wooden lift built for papal use, and Pope Clement VII's tiny frescoed bathroom by Giulio Romano.

The second and third floors house a collection of tapestry, paintings, and fresco. The terraces and café are popular destinations within the castle, and offer panoramic views of the nearby dome of St Peter's.

Ponte Sant'Angelo

Exit the Castel Sant'Angelo and cross over the Tiber river at the bustling footbridge of **Ponte Sant' Angelo ❷**. This is one of the prettiest bridges in the city. The decorated walk was made to Bernini's design in the 1680s, to revamp Hadrian's original bridge.

Traverse the zebra crossing, and continue straight along the Via del Banco di Santo Spirito until it opens onto the busy Corso Vittorio Emanuele II. Cross over to the tiny Via del Consolato and continue to the long and elegant Via Giulia, on the left.

VIA GIULIA

The street of **Via Giulia** is one of Rome's most prestigious addresses, dating from the early 16th century. Pope Julius II (best known for hiring Michelangelo to decorate the ceiling of the Sistine Chapel) commissioned the architect Donato Bramante, who was working on the plans for the new St Peter's, to create the first straight thoroughfare through the congested medieval alleys surrounding Campo de' Fiori. Walking down the Via Giulia now gives an impression of quiet elegance. The street is lined with small antique shops, chic art galleries, and piano bars nestled between palaces and church courtyards.

San Giovanni dei Fiorentini

Directly across from Via del Consolato, at the start of the Via Giulia, is the Florentine church of **San Giovanni dei**

Fiorentini ❸ (7.30am–1pm and 4–7 pm; free), started in 1509 and designed by papal architects Sangallo, Sansovino and della Porta. Inside is an impressive Baroque altar by Bernini's infamous rival Francesco Borromini.

Towards the Ponte Sisto

Heading southeast along the Via Giulia you pass some lovely examples

Above from far left: Castel Sant'Angelo, outside and inside; one of Bernini's angels on the Ponte Sant'Angelo; Via Giulia.

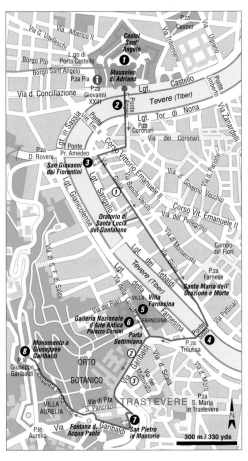

Tosca

Giacomo Puccini's lyrical opera *Tosca* is set against the backdrop of the Castel Sant'Angelo. It is from the great heights of the ramparts that the heroine, Tosca, dramatically jumps to her death.

of Renaissance palazzi. There are also some nice places to stop for a drink along the way, including **Coccodrillo**, see ①①.

On the right, down the Via del Gonfalone, is the **Oratorio di Santa Lucia del Gonfalone**, which often has summer concerts. Two streets down, turn right into the small Vicolo delle Prigioni (lane of the prisons), and you'll see the old prisons built in 1655 by Pope Innocent X Pamphilj.

Further along the Via Giulia on the right (directly across from the Via dei Farnesi) is the macabre church of **Santa Maria dell' Orazione e Morte** (St Mary of Prayer and Death).

At the end of the Via Giulia, just past the fountain of the **Mascherone** (big mask) is the footbridge of the **Ponte Sisto ④**, leading over the Tiber river.

MONTE DEL GIANICOLO

The current form of the Ponte Sisto was constructed in 1471 by Pope Sixtus IV as a grand entry into the neighbourhood of **Trastevere** *(see p.70)*.

Cross the Piazza Trilussa, and west of the piazza along the Via di Ponte Sisto turn right onto the Via della Lungara, passing through the arch of the Renaissance gateway of the **Porta Settimiana**.

Villa Farnesina

Look for the entrance to the stunning **Villa Farnesina ⑤** (Via della Lungara 230; tel: 06-6802 7268; Mon–Sat 9.30am–1pm; charge) to the right. This small but sumptuous villa was built in 1511 by the architect Baldassarre Peruzzi for the banking mogul Agostino Chigi, who was Pope Julius II's primary financier. The real treasure is Raphael's fresco on the ceiling of the open loggia. The story of *Cupid and Psyche* was chosen in honour of the wedding of Agostino Chigi, and the central scene depicts the marriage banquet, with figures surrounded by garlands of erotic fruits and vegetables. The upper floor has some lovely illusionistic perspectives by Peruzzi, with views of 16th-century Rome.

Palazzo Corsini

Across from the Farnesina is the **Palazzo Corsini**, housing the stunning **Galleria Nazionale d'Arte Antica ⑥** (National Gallery of Art; Via della Lungara 10; tel: 06-6880 2323; www.galleriaborghese.it; Tue–Sun

---

Food and Drink 🍴

① COCCODRILLO

Via Giulia 14; tel: 06-6819 2650; Thur–Tue 6.30pm–1am; €€–€€€
A stylish bar and restaurant which often has piano music or a small live band playing in the corner. The unusual menu serves updated Italian fusion, with dishes such as spaghetti with figs. Perfect for a drink or light dinner after an evening stroll.

② SICILIA AL TAPPO

Via Garibaldi 68; tel: 06-5833 5490; Tue–Sun noon–3pm, 7.30pm–midnight; €€
This bright restaurant is decorated with wooden tables and a mixture of southern ceramics, and offers an outdoor seating area in the summer. The menu is Sicilian with fish specialities and an extensive southern Italian wine list.

③ ANTICA PESA

Via Garibaldi 18; tel: 06-580 9236; Mon–Sat 7.30–11.30pm; €€€
Antica Pesa serves typical Roman dishes such as ravioli with a white truffle sauce as well as seasonal chef's specialities. The wine list is very good and the patio garden is perfect for relaxing and celebrity-spotting.

9am–7pm; charge). The palazzo was built for the Cardinal Riario in 1510, and completely rebuilt in 1736 under the ownership of Cardinal Corsini. It has housed numerous popes and members of nobility over the centuries. The Palazzo Corsini rivals any major art collection in Europe, and includes paintings by Caravaggio, Rubens, Van Dyck and Murillo to name only a few. The full collection is divided with the Palazzo Barberini *(see p.52)*.

Restaurant Options

Retrace your steps through the Porta Settimiana, turning right up the Via Giuseppe Garibaldi. Along this street are two great restaurants, convenient on either the ascent or the descent of the walk. **Sicilia al Tappo** is located near the bottom of the hill for re-fuelling before the climb, see ⑪②, or the more elegant **Antica Pesa** (evenings only), see ⑪③, near the summit.

San Pietro in Montorio and the Tempietto

Continue up Via Garibaldi to the church of Santa Maria dei Sette Dolori. To the right of the church is a stairway that brings you up to the piazza and the church of **San Pietro in Montorio** ❼ (tel: 06-581 3940; 8.30am–noon, 4–6pm; free). The current church was remodelled in the late 15th century by order from Ferdinand and Isabella of Spain, and includes many master works by Renaissance artists.

For a glimpse of the most visited monument at the church, look in to the narrow cloister. There you will find the perfectly constructed **Tempietto** built in 1502 by Bramante (courtyard of San Pietro in Montorio; tel: 06-581 3940; Tues–Sun 9.30am–12.30pm, 2–4pm; free; *see margin, right*).

Piazzale Giuseppe Garibaldi

Further up the hill is the crowning **Fontana dell'Acqua Paola** commissioned by the Pope Paul V Borghese in 1612, in honour of the grand reopening of the ancient aqueduct built by Emperor Trajan in 109. Continue along the upper route of the Paseggiata di Gianicolo to see some of Rome's most breathtaking views from the terrace of **Piazzale Giuseppe Garibaldi** ❽. The monument commemorates General Garibaldi's achievements in fending off the French troops on the Gianicolo Hill in 1849.

To descend from the heights either continue along the Paseggiata di Gianicolo, arriving at the far side of the hill near the Vatican, or retrace your steps down to Trastevere.

Above from far left: follow the Via Garibaldi up the Gianicolo; monument to Garibaldi; Villa Farnesina; sunset view from Piazzale Giuseppe Garibaldi.

Tiny Temple
The Tempietto, or tiny temple, is considered the first building of the Renaissance. Despite its small scale, the design follows ideal symmetry and classical proportions. It was built to mark the traditional spot of St Peter's martyrdom.

Botanical Gardens

The formal Orto Botanico (Largo Cristina di Svezia 24; tel: 06-4991 7106; Mon–Sat 9.30am–6.30pm; charge) dates from the 1880s, and was structured out of the 17th-century gardens of the Palazzo Corsini. The stepped and terraced gardens are still in existence and have an amazing array of exotic and rare plants as well as historic species. A series of lovely tiered fountains can be found along the hidden paths leading up the hill. Maintenance of the gardens was taken over by the University of Rome in 1983.

JEWISH QUARTER AND TRASTEVERE

This walk connects two of Rome's most characterful medieval neighbourhoods: the Jewish Quarter, with its ancient Roman roots, and lively Trastevere, with its bohemian heart. Both have been home to fringe cultures for centuries.

DISTANCE 3km (2 miles)
TIME A half day
START Largo di Torre Argentina
END Piazza Trilussa
POINTS TO NOTE

Trastevere, where this route ends, is an ideal place for an evening drink or dinner. Consider this walk for an afternoon, have lunch en route, and finish as the neighbourhood comes to life.

Food and Drink

① DA GIGGETTO

Via del Portico d'Ottavia 21; tel: 06-686 1105; Tue–Sun 12.30–3pm, 7–11.30pm; €€
Da Giggetto has the feel of a retro film set. It has a diverse enough menu for any tastes, yet still focuses on Roman traditional dishes, of which the signature is crispy artichokes. The huge seating area is always crowded.

What's a Ghetto?

The term 'ghetto' is Venetian in origin and in Italian is not generally used with any negative connotations. In Rome it indicates the quarter between the Monte dei Cenci and the Teatro di Marcello, once walled in by the papacy in 1556. The area was known from the medieval period as the Campo Judeorum, after many Jews moved across the river from Trastevere.

TORRE ARGENTINA

The route begins at the centre of the traffic-clogged **Largo di Torre Argentina ❶**, a fascinating open piazza with a subterranean archaeological area called the **Area Sacra dell' Argentina**. The remains of the four visible temples were only discovered and actively excavated in the 1920s. The oldest section is from the temple of Juturna and dates to the 3rd century BC, while the newest section was built as part of the nearby Theatre of Pompey *(see p.41)*. This area gives some impression of the scale of ancient Roman buildings and the level of the original streets. At the southwest side are the headquarters of the volunteer cat sanctuary *(see box, p.71)*, whose inhabitants can be found draped about the ancient ruins.

JEWISH QUARTER

Leave the piazza from the southeast corner along little Via Paganica. This will bring you to the northern edge of the Jewish ghetto *(see margin, left)*. The small neighbourhood is still home to one of Europe's oldest communities of Jewish families, many of whom have been Romans for centuries, surviving religious persecution and the Holocaust.

The street opens onto the diminutive Piazza Mattei with the restored **Fontana delle Tartarughe ❷** (Fountain of the Tortoises), completed in 1585 according to designs by Giacomo della Porta.

Head east along the Via dei Funari into the characteristic twisting lanes of

---

the ghetto; keep right at the piazza, following the Vicolo di Campitelli, through the arch and onto the back of the Teatro di Marcello *(see p.35)*.

Portico d'Ottavia

Coming around the archaeological area dominated by the Teatro di Marcello, you will find the ruined **Portico d'Ottavia ❸**, a gate built by Augustus in honour of his sister Ottavia, the unlucky wife of Marc Antony. By the 18th century the ruins of the Portico were home to the local fish market, and it is recognisable in many genre paintings of the period.

There are several great restaurants here including **Da Giggetto**, with tables overlooking the square, see ⑪①.

Palazzo Cenci

Cross the piazza created along the Via del Portico d'Ottavia into the heart of the Jewish Quarter, to the **Piazza delle Cinque Scole ❹**, recognisable by the basin fountain located at the back of the **Palazzo Cenci**. The palace was once home to the powerful Cenci dynasty, whose complicated tragedies were written about in Percy Bysshe Shelley's drama *The Cenci*.

Above from far left: Area Sacra dell' Argentina; three snapshots of the Jewish Quarter.

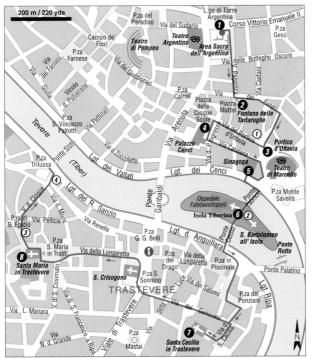

Below: Fountain of the Tortoises; entrance to the synagogue.

River Cruising

Rome's river life can be enjoyed from the water itself on a Tiber river cruise (Battelli di Roma, tel: 06-9774 5496; www.rexervation.com/crociere.asp). Boats depart from the southeast bank near the Ponte Sant'Angelo. A hop-on/hop-off service can be caught at the Calata Anguillara stop on Tiber Island.

Synagogue

Head east away from the palace; at the end of the Via Catalana is the **Sinagoga** ❺ (Synagogue; Lungotevere dei Cenci; tel: 06-6840 0661; www.museoebraico.roma.it; Sun–Thur 9.30am–4.40pm, Fri 9am–2pm; charge). This relatively new addition to the area was constructed in 1904, after the Unification of Italy, as a symbol of newfound freedom. The confining walls of the ghetto were torn down under the new Republic. The unusual square dome above the synagogue is made of aluminium; inside, the decoration is in the Liberty Style (Art Nouveau). The Synagogue Museum schedules hourly tours of the synagogue, with an overview of the history of the Roman Jewish community.

TIBER ISLAND

Cross over the Lungotevere dei Cenci and make your way over the oldest-standing bridge in Rome, the **Ponte**

Fabricio (built in 62 BC). You will come to the boat-shaped **Isola Tiberina** ❻ (Tiber Island), the smallest inhabited island in the world. An ancient temple to Aesculapius, the Greek god of medicine, once stood on the island, marking the auspicious location for healing. There has been a church and hospital on this site for centuries.

In the middle of the island is the wonderful trattoria **Sora Lella**, see ⑪②. During the summer, the wide sloping banks are home to festivals, outdoor eateries and lively beer gardens. From the south side of this lower level it is possible to see the ancient **Ponte Rotto** (Broken Bridge), the beautifully carved remains of Rome's first stone bridge.

TRASTEVERE

Leaving the island, cross into Trastevere, meaning 'across the Tevere' (the Italian name for the Tiber river). This independent neighbourhood still has the feel of old Roman tradition mixed with a laid-back left-wing culture, reflected in its artisan workshops, hanging laundry, and rough wooden tables set up on the pavement. Many of the street names here reflect their original function.

Santa Cecilia in Trastevere

From the Ponte Cestio turn left, and then turn right and head past the car park along the Via Titta Scarpetta (Street of the Ladies' Slippers) to the Via dei Salumi (Street of Salami). Turn left here and take the second right, Via Vascellari. Continue until you reach the church of **Santa Cecilia in Trastevere**

Food and Drink

② SORA LELLA

Via di Ponte Quattro Capi 16; tel: 06-6897 4063; closed Sun; €€€
This well-known upmarket trattoria continues to be packed for lunch and dinner. They serve a combination of traditional Roman fare with a refined twist.

③ OMBRE ROSSE

Piazza di Sant'Egidio 12; tel: 06-588 4155; 9am–1am; €
Attractive dark wood, nice outdoor seating and a great selection of long drinks makes this perfect for a break. Small menu, too.

④ CAFÉ FRIENDS

Piazza Trilussa, 34; tel: 06-581 6111; 11am–2.30am; €
Modern and buzzing, serving coffees, cocktails, sandwiches and buffet food at most times of the day. Great for sipping a pre-dinner drink while you watch the world go by in the piazza outside.

7. This late-4th-century church is dedicated St Cecilia, one of the early martyrs. The current structure dates primarily from the 12th century, with some original elements, and the interior has several impressive mosaics from the period. Look out for the fragmentary *Last Judgement* frescoes by Pietro Cavallini in the galley, and an incredible Baroque sculpture of *Santa Cecilia* by Stefano Maderno below the altar.

Heart of Trastevere

Double back along the Via di Santa Cecilia, then turn left along the Via dei Genovesi. When you reach the busy Viale di Trastevere, turn right and then left past the church of San Crisogano into the bustling Via della Lungaretta. This road acts as the main thoroughfare into central Trastevere, and the street performers, vendors and outdoor pizzerie spill out into the large piazza at the end. This well-used square with its bubbling fountains is the real heart of the neighbourhood.

Santa Maria in Trastevere

The focal point of the piazza is the tranquil basilica of **Santa Maria in Trastevere** **8** (tel: 06-581 4802; 7am–12.30pm, 1.30–8pm; free), a good place to find a moment of serenity in the middle of the busy city. It is one of the earliest Christian churches, dating from the 3rd century, although, like many others in Rome, it was rebuilt in the 12th century. Inside the incongruous 18th-century portico is a wall covered in fragments of ancient marble plaques. The beautiful granite columns along the

nave were taken as spoils from the Baths of Caracalla *(see p.33)*. The mosaics of the Virgin Mary on the front of the church give some idea of the style and quality of the decoration within. Of note are the sparkling apse mosaics that complement Cavallini's series of the *Life of the Virgin* dating to 1291. The Byzantine influence imparts a subtle balance between stylised figures and animals, and heartfelt expression.

Places to Hang Out

There are many good restaurants, cafés and bars in this area. To sit and people watch, wander over to the Piazza di Sant'Egidio to a table at the **Ombre Rosse**, see 🍽③, or continue further along the pretty Vicolo de' Cinque to the student-filled **Piazza Trilussa** at the edge of the river. The modern **Café Friends**, see 🍽④, is a great stopping point any time of day.

Above from far left: Tiber Island; the facade of Santa Maria in Trastevere; buildings on the piazza named after the church.

Below: Trastevere transport.

The Cats of Rome

Rome is home to hundreds of thousands of stray cats living in its ruins. They have been remarked upon and painted or photographed for generations. In recent years the cats have been counted, fed, vaccinated and neutered through a volunteer charity service at Largo di Torre Argentina. The animal care runs on international donations, and many cats are available for adoption.

Cats seen around the city with a clipped ear indicate that they are cared for by the Torre Argentina group. (Cat Sanctuary at the Area Sacra dell'Argentina; tel: 06-687 2133; www.romancats.com; noon–6pm.)

AVENTINO AND TESTACCIO

Just south of the Capitoline Hill are the quarters of Aventino and Testaccio.
Centrally located, rich in history, and surprisingly off the beaten track, the
Aventine Hill, with its great setting and cool breezes, looks over Testaccio,
known for its markets and nightlife.

Sour Oranges

During the expansion of the Roman Empire, civic pride was expressed through the construction of illustrious palaces, temples, open squares, and of course gardens. Exotic plants were imported from all over the world to decorate the outdoor 'rooms', and streets were planted with flower and fruit trees for a festive look. To deter theft, a special orange was developed that produced fruit all year but was also completely inedible. The decorative sour orange is still grown in many public spaces in Rome.

DISTANCE 4km (2½ miles)

TIME A half day

START Circo Massimo metro

END Centrale Montemartini

POINTS TO NOTE

This itinerary, though not difficult, covers a lot of ground. Consider stopping for lunch along the way or picking up a picnic at the food market in Testaccio. The route ends with the wonderful Centrale Montemartini museum; though located along an industrial boulevard, it is well connected for a return journey to the centre. There are many buses that pass directly in front of the museum, or the metro (Piramide) is only a 7–10 minute walk north.

This walk starts with a breath of fresh air on the aristocratic Aventine Hill. After admiring the serene churches and views, the route continues into the working-class neighbourhood of Testaccio, one of the city's most dynamic areas. It doesn't feature on most tourist itineraries but it's worth a visit before it goes the way of Trastevere and becomes trendy, changing its character for good.

AVENTINO

Starting at the metro station named after the **Circo Massimo** *(see p.33)*, head northwest along the Via del Circo Massimo to the circular Piazzale Ugo La Malfa. The Via di Valle Murcia leads up the Aventino through a rose garden. The Aventino is officially one of the seven hills of Rome, and has been inhabited by patrician families since the age of the Republic. Some of the regal feeling is retained in its leafy streets and walled gardens, and the chaos of the nearby traffic has not yet overwhelmed this hilltop oasis.

Parco Savello and Santa Sabina

At the summit of the slope is the church of Santa Sabina. In front is the Piazza Pietro d'Illiria (used as a car park), on the right of which is an arched entry into the beautiful **orangery ❶** (Giardino degli Aranci), also known as the **Parco Savello**. The garden was once part of the Savello family fortress of the 12th century. Now it is full of families with small children and couples having photos taken under the orange trees *(see margin, left)*.

The adjacent church of **Santa Sabina** ❷ (Piazza Pietro d'Illiria 1; tel: 06-5794 0600; 7am–12.30pm, 3.30–7pm; free) is one of the most popular wedding locations in the city. The 5th-century interior is quite simple, with a light airy feeling created by the open space, and beautifully set Corinthian columns and clear glass windows. The rare cypress wood doors from the 420s (at the left entry) show scenes from the New Testament, depicting one of the first known representations of the crucifixion. In the portico are several inscribed floor tombs, made from ancient marble sarcophagi. This early method of recycling, which can be seen in medieval churches throughout Rome, preserved the original carvings; a clever rotating stand allows for viewing both sides.

Priory of Malta and Sant' Anselmo

At the far end of the summit is the Piazza dei Cavalieri di Malta (Knights of Malta) with its cypress-lined wall. On the piazza is the **Priorato di Malta** ❸. This secretive chivalric order was founded in 1050, and continues to operate as a charitable organization. The Priory is closed to the public, but the main draw is their keyhole. Take a peek through it and you'll see the far-away dome of St Peter's appear as if it were in the garden. The piazza and the doorway were designed by the fantastical 18th-century printmaker, Gian Battista Piranesi.

The monastic building at the far side of the piazza is the church of **Sant' Anselmo** ❹ (Piazza Cavalieri di Malta 5; tel: 06-579 1356; www-sant anselmo.net; Tues–Sun 9am–noon, 4–7pm; free), constructed in 1900 as the seat of the Rule of St Benedict. The architecture is a strange mixture of neo-Gothic and Romanesque.

Perhaps the most interesting thing is the **Benedictine shop** *(see church hours)*, which sells teas, medicinal herbs, liqueurs and honeys produced by the Benedictines. The monks sing Gregorian-style vespers at sunset on most evenings as well as on Sunday mornings.

Above from far left: the orangery, or Parco Savello; door to the Priory of Malta – take a peek through the keyhole; fountain at the church of Santa Sabina; the church itself.

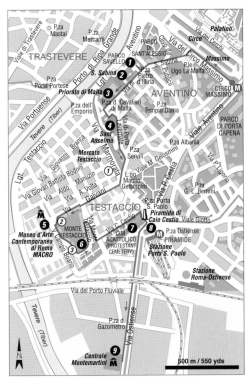

TESTACCIO

Take the Via di Porta Lavernale to drop down into Testaccio. Continue to the foot of the hill and cross the clogged artery of the Via Marmorata to Via Galvani. A few streets up Via Marmorata is the family-run **Gastronomia Volpetti**, one of the best Italian delicatessens in the city, see ⑪①. Just around the corner from Volpetti is the **Mercato Testaccio** in the Piazza Testaccio, the main daily produce market of the area, and also one of the best.

Monte Testaccio

Continue along the Via Galvani past several trendy nightclubs and bars. There is a noticeable contrast between the solemn hillside of the Aventino, and the flat regular lanes of the Testaccio. Most of the current residential Testaccio was built in the 19th century, but like all of Rome it has an older history. The neighbourhood is named after the **Monte Testaccio** (Hill of Shards), which is a 35-m (115-ft)-high hill created from bits of broken pottery. The low-lying flats of the area were used from 140 BC to about AD 250 to unload the millions of amphorae and supplies coming up river to the capital. When the great jars of olive oil were decanted they were flung onto the pile. The function of the neighbourhood as a major gateway for food and goods lasted until the mid-1970s when the city's congestion forced suppliers to the outlying suburbs.

Mattatoio and MACRO

At the end of the street is the entrance to what was once the **Mattatoio** (slaughterhouse) of Rome. The massive complex closed in 1975 and was abandoned for over a decade. The eerie architecture and uncharacteristic warehouse spaces are now home to Roma Tre (University of Rome), the Villagio Globale (a summer venue for arts, music, and fringe gay scene), and the **Museo d'Arte Contemporanea di Roma** or **MACRO** ❺ (Piazza Orazio Giustiniani 4; tel: 06-6710 7040; www. macro.roma.museum; Tue–Sun 4pm– midnight; charge). The space exhibits edgy, and often unknown, contemporary artists and is one of the few venues for performance and installation art.

Across from the entrance of MACRO is **Acqua e Farina**, a relaxed restaurant serving delicious food, see ⑪②.

Watery Grave
Both Keats and Shelley died within a year of each other while living in Italy. Keats died of tuberculosis in Rome in 1821, and Shelley drowned the following year off the coast of La Spezia. The ominous epitaph on Keats's grave reads 'Here lies One Whose Name was writ in Water.' His name is not actually mentioned on the stone (see below).

Via Monte Testaccio

From the Via Galvani, head south. Where the road forks, turn left into the **Via Monte Testaccio ❻**. There are several clubs and bars along this street that have been literally carved out of the millions of shards of pottery which make up the hillside.

One of the better restaurants of the area, **Trattoria Checchino dal 1887**, see ⑪③, specialises in meat dishes (it used to be next to the slaughterhouse) and also has plenty of ancient amphorae in their wine cellar to look at.

Protestant Cemetery and the Pyramid

At the far side turn right onto Via Nicola Zabaglia and left to the Via Caio Cestio to reach the Cimitero Acattolico, known as the **Protestant Cemetery ❼** (tel: 06-574 1900; www.protestant cemetery.it; Mon–Sat 9am–5pm, Sun 9am–1pm; charge). This dilapidated burial ground has been a favourite of anglophiles since the 19th century. The most famous graves are those of the romantic poets John Keats and Percy Bysshe Shelley *(see margin, left)*.

At one edge of the cemetery is Rome's pyramid, known as the **Piramide di Caio Cestio ❽**. This attractive monument was constructed as a mausoleum for Caius Cestius in 18 BC, at a time when Egyptian decoration was the fashion.

Centrale Montemartini

Just to the south is Via Ostiense. Take a ten-minute walk down this road and you come to one of Rome's most intriguing museums. The road itself is built up and unappealing, but the rewards at the end are worth making the effort.

The **Centrale Montemartini ❾** (Via Ostiense 106; tel: 06-574 8042; www.centralemontemartini.org; Tue–Sun 9am–7pm; charge) is a fantastic marriage of art and technology, old and new; ancient sculpture is exhibited in a converted power station. The museum opened in 1997 as a temporary exhibition space for 400 sculptures from the Capitoline Museums. Use of the abandoned 1894 electrical plant was part of a larger overhaul of the Testaccio area that included the slaughterhouse, gasometer and general markets. The exhibition was so successful that it has become a permanent extension of the museums. The overall effect is mesmerising.

Above from far left: graffitied bus in Testaccio; Piramide di Caio Cestio; MACRO.

Below: street art; inhabitants of Testaccio are said to be the most loyal supporters of Roma football team.

Food and Drink

① GASTRONOMIA VOLPETTI
Via Marmorata 47; tel: 06-574 2352; www.volpetti.com; 8am–6pm; €–€€€
This delicatessen has some of the finest meats, cheeses and pastas in the city but it is takeaway only.

② ACQUA E FARINA
Piazza Giustiniani 2; tel: 06-574 1382; 12.30–2.30pm, 7.30–11.30pm; €€
A young and vibrant crowd fills this neighbourhood restaurant. Their dishes are often made with pizza dough cooked in inventive ways. The result is a modern twist on an old classic. Try the vegetable tarts or the cheese sticks.

③ TRATTORIA CHECCHINO DAL 1887
Via Monte Testaccio 30; tel: 06-574 6318; Tue–Sat; €€€
It is best to reserve here, as a steady stream of regulars come for the exceptional meat dishes. The wine list is top, but the fun part is going down into the cantina to have a look around.

SAN GIOVANNI AND ESQUILINO

The neighbouring areas of San Giovanni and the Esquiline hill are home to some of the most beautiful and historically important churches in the city, including the unassuming San Clemente, tiny Santa Prassede, imposing San Giovanni in Laterano and crowning Santa Maria Maggiore.

Cult of Mithras
Mithraism was a popular religious cult introduced to Rome through the legions in Asia Minor. It spanned most of the Roman Empire from Syria to Britain. Practices were associated with bull sacrifice and masculine potency, making it popular with military forces, but the fundamental beliefs shared uncanny similarities with Christianity. Mithraism was followed from the 1st century BC until it was banned under the edict of Theodosius I in 394.

Below: detail from San Clemente's apse.

DISTANCE 2.5km (1½ miles)
TIME A half day
START San Clemente
END Santa Maria Maggiore
POINTS TO NOTE
If this walk is started in the morning, it can easily be followed by walk 13 for a full day. If you choose to start in the afternoon, consider having lunch first in the Colosseum or San Clemente area.

Food and Drink

① PIZZERIA LE NAUMACHIE
Via Celimontana 7; tel: 06-700 2764; daily 12.30–11.30pm; €–€€
A consistently good pasta and wood-oven pizza place near the Colosseum. A very large seating area on the lower floor makes it good for an inexpensive meal with kids or big groups.

② RISTORANTE AI TRE SCALINI
Via del SS. Quattro 30; tel: 06-709 6309; daily noon–3pm, 7pm–midnight; €€–€€€
Tre Scalini is an excellent lunch or dinner choice in an area generally known for mediocre food. Wonderful fresh pasta dishes and grilled meats or fish; delicious lobster ravioli. Good wine list, too.

The walk starts behind the Colosseum at San Clemente, and continues to San Giovanni in Laterano, the world's ecumenical mother church. There are several good choices for lunch spots in the San Clemente area such as **Pizzeria Le Naumachie**, see ①①, or **Ai Tre Scalini**, see ①②.

SAN CLEMENTE

The unpretentious basilica of **San Clemente ①** (main entrance Piazza San Clemente; tel: 06-774 0021; www.basilicasanclemente.com; Mon–Sat 9am–12.30pm, 3–6pm, Sun noon–6pm; free; charge for excavations) is an open door into one of Rome's best time capsules. Its walls contain three separate houses of worship, built one upon the other and spanning a period of nearly two thousand years. The street-level building dates to the 12th century, incorporating some 6th-century sections, and has been run by an order of Irish Dominicans since the 17th century.

Not to be missed are the large apse mosaics from the 1180s; these depict the *Triumph of the Cross* as a twisting tree of life. In front of the altar is the

6th-century choir enclosure with lovely inlaid marble. The recently restored Renaissance chapel to St Catherine of Alexandria contains fine 15th-century frescoes by Masolino (best known for his collaboration on the Brancacci Chapel in Florence).

Lower Levels

Through the gift shop are the stairs down to the excavations (tickets can be purchased here). At the lower level is the original 4th-century church, with well-preserved fragments of the 11th-century frescoes depicting the miracles of St Clement. Further down, lit by bizarre modern torches, are an intact late 2nd-century temple to the pagan god Mithras *(see margin)*, and the adjacent apartments used for clandestine Christian worship. The constant sound of rushing water is the Cloaca Maxima, or ancient sewer, which is still in use.

SAN GIOVANNI

From the San Clemente area pick up the walk along the Via di San Giovanni in Laterano to the busy piazza at the side of the Lateran Palaces. These palaces were the first official papal residences and were used from the 4th century until the development of the Vatican complex *(see p.58)*.

San Giovanni in Laterano

Continue around Rome's largest standing obelisk, brought from the Temple of Amun at Karnak to decorate the *spina* (central spine) of the Circus Maximus. On the opposite side of the cluster of buildings, facing east, is the front of the basilica of **San Giovanni in Laterano** ❷ (tel: 06-6988 6433; 7am–6.30pm; free).

San Giovanni is officially the first Christian basilica, and the cathedral of the diocese of Rome, of which the Pope is bishop. As it houses the papal throne, the church holds a higher spiritual significance than St Peter's itself. San Giovanni is officially dedicated to Our

Above from far left: San Clemente; the church's ceiling; San Giovanni in Laterano.

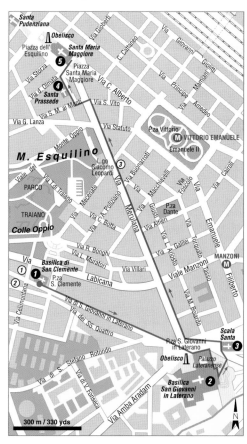

Saviour and also to St John the Baptist and St John the Evangelist.

The church has a rich history and many highlights. At the main entrance, in the bold 18th-century façade, are the original bronze doors, taken from the Curia in the Forum. The grand structure has been rebuilt multiple times throughout the ages, and the wonderful interior decorations reflect various phases of rebuilding. Do not miss the illustrious side chapels built by many of Rome's noble families. The massive Baroque statues of the 12 Apostles line the support columns of the nave and contrast with the 14th-century baldacchino covering the papal altar. The gilt-and-coffered-wood ceiling dates to 1567. Away from the grand scale of the main church is the calming **cloister** (daily 9am–6pm; charge), which dates to 1230 and is decorated in the Cosmatesque style.

Below: the ancient bronze doors of San Giovanni in Laterano *(see also p.8–9).*

International Esquilino

The Renaissance villas that once covered the Esquiline were sadly demolished in the 1870s to make way for Rome's new showcase neighbourhood, with the focal point being the grand Piazza Vittorio Emanuele II, named after the new king. The plan failed to attract the growing middle classes, and it fell into decline leaving an area still known for its shabby apartments and run-down hotels. Because of low property values, the neighbourhood is now home to a thriving international community, and the new Chinese and Asian population is slowly carving out a niche on the Esquiline. The busy outdoor vegetable and fish market, at Via Lamarmora, behind the train station, is now run by many of the immigrant families. Typical Italian fresh produce and goods have been replaced with halal meats, spices and exotic African fruits.

Scala Santa

Across the piazza is the entrance to the **Scala Santa** ❸ (Piazza San Giovanni in Laterano; Apr–Sept daily 6.30am–noon, 3–6pm, Oct–Mar 3.30–6.45pm; free), believed to be the 28 steps Christ ascended in Pontius Pilate's house. The Emperor Constantine's mother, St Helena, brought the stairs to Rome as one of the first holy relics. Busloads of devout pilgrims still climb up on their knees.

ESQUILINO

Just north of the obelisk is the long, tree-lined Via Merulana, which runs up the western slope of the Esquiline, the highest of Rome's seven hills. This residential area is full of shops selling cheeses, cured meats, furniture and edible gifts made by monks to support their religious orders (Dispensa degli Scalzi at no. 254). The bakery **Panella**, see ⑪③, is perfect for a snack along the way.

Santa Prassede

Towards the top of the road, turn left at Via San Martino ai Monti, then right onto the Via Santa Prassede, and you will reach the unassuming **Santa Prassede** ❹ (tel: 06-488 2456; daily 8am–noon, 4–6pm; free) at no. 9. This lovely little church is a hidden treasure. Dating to 780, it is dedicated to one of the daughters of St Pudens, who was St Paul's first convert to Christianity. The intricate Byzantine-style mosaics depicting the sainted family are not only enchant-

ing, but are also some of the earliest and most important in Rome. Nearby is the church of Santa Pudenziana, Santa Prassede's sister *(see p.82)*.

Santa Maria Maggiore

Just round the corner is **Santa Maria Maggiore** ❺ (tel: 06-483 195; daily 7am–7pm; free), one of four patriarchal basilicas, and the only one dedicated to the Virgin Mary. In the piazza at the front of the church is a massive column with a bronze statue of the Virgin and Child, dating to 1615; the column is from the Basilica of Constantine in the Forum.

The various decorative styles of Santa Maria Maggiore give the church a feeling of regal elegance. Most notable among them are the rich Cosmatesque floors reminiscent of prayer rugs from Byzantium. To the left, near the altar, is the elaborate chapel to Pope Paul V Borghese, with a Baroque altar containing one of the oldest icons of the Virgin Mary.

The mosaics in the main church are exceptional, with a series form the 430s located along the nave depicting stories form the Old Testament. These are located near the upper windows, and do not follow chronological order.

The nave decoration is complemented by the powerful *Coronation of the Virgin* apse mosaics from 1295, by Jacopo Torriti. The expansive wood coffered ceiling was added by Pope Alexander VI Borgia in the 1490s and is decorated with the first gold brought back from the New World by the voyages of Christopher Columbus.

In the confession, below the high altar, are the relics of the Holy Manger from Bethlehem. Many of the familiar Christmas traditions celebrated today originated at Santa Maria Maggiore.

Interestingly, the rear side of this church is decorated with a magnificent staircase and one of Rome's many Egyptian obelisks. The obelisk at the centre of the Piazza Esquilino is from the Mausoleum of Augustus *(see p.42)*.

Food and Drink

③ PANELLA

Via Merulana 55; Mon–Fri 8am–2pm, 5–8pm, closed Thur afternoons; €
This wonderful neighbourhood bakery sells breads, cakes, lovely biscuits, crepes, savoury filo bundles and mini pizzas, as well as coffee. Perfect for a takeaway bite.

Above from far left: nave of San Giovanni in Laterano; Scala Santa building and statuary; looking towards Santa Maria Maggiore.

Miracle of the Snow
Every August 5th, thousands of white flower petals are showered from the roof of Santa Maria Maggiore during mass. This is in commemoration of the legendary snowfall that fell on Esquiline Hill in the year 352.

Left: Santa Maria Maggiore.

DIOCLETIAN COMPLEX AND MONTI

This walk starts with the national archaeological collections at the Baths of Diocletian, then continues down into the ancient streets of the Rione Monti (hilly district), and leads up to the pilgrim church of San Pietro in Vincoli.

DISTANCE 3km (2 miles)
TIME A half day
START Diocletian Complex
END San Pietro in Vincoli
POINTS TO NOTE

This is a an easy walk incorporating several archaeological collections. The starting point is located only a few streets away from walk 12, and the two walks can be paired for a full day itinerary. Two of the museums comprising the Museo Nazionale Romano are covered in this route. Tickets are valid for all four museums over a three day period.

Below: classical sculptures at the Baths of Diocletian.

DIOCLETIAN COMPLEX

Rome's richest collection of archaeological artefacts has been housed in the remains of the **Terme di Diocleziano** since the 1870s. The **Museo Nazionale Romano ❶** (National Museum of Rome; Viale Enrico de Nicola 79; tel: 06-3996 7700; www.pierreci.it; Tue–Sun 9am–7.45pm; charge) shares its collections with three other spaces, the nearby Palazzo Massimo, Palazzo Altemps, and the Crypta Balbi. The most historic group of artefacts is

exhibited in the ruins of the magnificent *terme*, or bath complex.

History of the Baths

Built by the Emperor Diocletian in 306, the baths served up to 3,000 visitors at one time. In addition to the requisite bathing areas, heated to different temperatures with elaborate subterranean chambers, there were rooms for steam and a large *natatio* (open air pool). The ambitious *terme* had separate spaces for meetings, dining, shopping, lecturing, temples, art exhibitions, and a library. These great ruins were first remodeled by Michelangelo in the 1560s, under Pope Pius IV. Michelangelo's construction of a Carthusian monastery kept much of the original structure as it was, and his cloister still creates a focal point for the space.

The Collection

The complex houses over 400 classical sculptures and architectural fragments. When entering from the Via Enrico Fermi (across the street from the Termini Station) you will see the gardens and cloister with signs indicating open sections. Rooms I–IX contain temple statuary and decorations from the baths themselves. Rooms X–XII house

major works such as the *Anadyomene Aphrodite* and the *Lance-Bearer*, and an extensive epigraph collection.

Santa Maria degli Angeli

Exiting along the Viale Luigi Einaudi brings you to the brick entrance of the church of **Santa Maria degli Angeli** 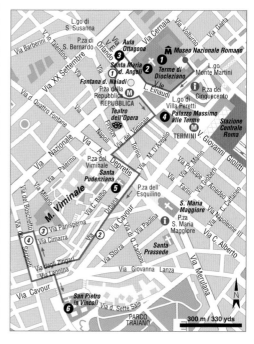❷ (Piazza della Repubblica; tel: 06-488 0812; www.santamariadegliangeli roma.it; 7am–6.30pm; free). The unusual façade is a section of Diocletian's massive complex, decorated with very modern bronze doors. The church was part of the 1563 construction plan by Michelangelo, who cleverly created a vaulted transept out of the existing *frigidarium* (cool water bath). His architectural scheme left the original structure exposed and he incorporated even the massive granite columns into the church. Remodelling in 1749 greatly modified Michelangelo's idea but the scale of the building remains. On the floor, running diagonally, is the meridian line added in 1702 by Francesco Bianchini under Pope Clement XI. This was designed to check the accuracy of the new Gregorian reformation of the calendar.

Octagonal Hall

Past Santa Maria degli Angeli is the entrance to the **Aula Ottagona** ❸ (Octagonal Hall; 9am–2pm, free), one of the few standing sections of the bath complex. The room has an octagonal oculus and was transformed into the planetarium in 1928. It now houses some of the most elegant classical sculptures from the nearby museum.

Cross the Piazza della Repubblica, circling around the beautiful **Fontana delle Naiadi** (Fountain of the Naiads) designed by Mario Rutelli *(see margin, right)*. The Via delle Terme di Diocleziano at the far side leads to the entrance of the Palazzo Massimo.

Snack Break

You may be tempted to stop at one of the many cafés. They are all more or less similar in quality and price. For a real treat backtrack along the Via Emanuele Orlando to **Dagnino**, one of Rome's legendary spots specialising in Sicilian pastry, see ⑪① *(on p.83)*. Continue along to the Palazzo Massimo.

Above from far left: scenes from the Diocletian Complex.

Naked Naiads

When the Fountain of the Naiads was designed in 1901 it was met with instant censorship. The sensual nature of the plump nymphs was considered too risqué and a fence was quickly erected to conceal them.

Below: exhibits at the Palazzo Massimo.

Below: clothes boutique in Monti.

PALAZZO MASSIMO

The majority of the collections of the Museo Nazionale Romano are on view at the **Palazzo Massimo alle Terme** ❹ (Largo di Villa Peretti 1; tel: 06-480 201; www.pierreci.it; Tue–Sun 9am–7.45pm; charge; tickets from the Terme di Diocleziano are valid). The museum opened in 1889 and the antiquities collections span a period from the 2nd century BC through the 4th century AD. After extensive remodelling in the early 1990s, it has emerged as one of the world's leading Classical art museums.

The collections are arranged thematically. On the lower floor is the numismatic section and the ground floor is dedicated to statuary, including a lovely bust of *Hadrian*, and the famous *Via Labicana Augustus*. Statuary continues on the first floor with statues of gods from Nero's summer villa, and Roman copies of Greek originals showing the influence of the Hellenistic styles. Most impressive are the rooms on the second floor with lively frescoes from the villa of Augustus's wife Livia.

RIONE MONTI

To continue, walk southwest along the Via Viminale, past the **Teatro dell' Opera**, Rome's primary opera house, producing both lively classics and new productions, to the Piazza del Viminale (home to the Ministry of Internal Affairs).

At the end of the street turn left. The descent along Via Augusto Depretis leads into the neighbourhood of Monti. This ancient residential area was once called the *Suburra (see margin, right)*, and was renamed in the Middle Ages for its location between the Viminale, Esquiline and Quirinal hills. Now it is considered one of the most authentically Roman areas, with tiny alleyways and cobbled lanes. Well-heeled Romans can be seen out lunching or shopping in one of the many little boutiques. Some of the charm was wiped away under Benito Mussolini who had about 30 per cent of Monti flattened to create the Via dei Foro Imperiali, but the feel of the neighbourhood remains.

Santa Pudenziana

At the Piazza dell'Esquilino, where you can see the rear of Santa Maria Maggiore *(see p.79)*, take the first right. Along Via Urbana is the tiny church of **Santa Pudenziana** ❺ (Via Urbana 160; tel: 06-481 4622; 8am-noon, 3-6pm; free) located down the stairs at the old street level. The church is dedicated to the daughter of Pudens, a 1st-century

senator. According to legend Pudens hosted St Peter, and he and his two daughters, Pudenziana and Prassede, became early Christian converts. The church of Santa Prassede is located nearby on the Esquiline *(see p. 78)*. Both churches have lovely 4th-century early Christian decoration. The apse mosaics at Santa Pudenziana have been through several bouts of questionable restoration, but the scene depicting the Apostles in Roman togas is still mesmerising.

Shopping and Food Options

Continue down the hill along Via Urbana with its tiny workshops, mosaic studios, and shirt makers. Consider stopping for a break. Stylish **Urbana 47** is perfect for a sampling of local wines by the glass, see ⑪②.

If something more substantial is in order, turn right into the Via degli Zingari (street of the gypsies), then take the second right, the Via del Boschetto. This straight road is jammed with antique stores, boutiques and trendy designers. **La Carbonara** on Via Panisperna is the best choice for a meal, see ⑪③, or try the light fare at **Ai Tre Scalini**, see ⑪④.

To continue the route turn left into Via Panisperna and left again into Via dei Serpenti, which is considered the 'main street' of Monti. Head past the junction with Via degli Zingari, and turn left into Via Leonina. This will take you past typical local shops to a set of steps along the right. Climb the steps, cross the busy Via Cavour, and continue up the steps and through the archway on the far side.

SAN PIETRO IN VINCOLI

The Baroque style of the church of **San Pietro in Vincoli** ❻ (St Peter in Chains; Piazza San Pietro in Vincoli; tel: 06-488 2865; 7am–noon, 3.30–7pm; free) gives no indication of the popularity of this spot. Visitors come either to look at the reliquary housing the chains used to bind St Peter in the Mamertine Prison, or to see Michelangelo's unfinished monument to Pope Julius II. The figure of Moses, one of the proposed 47 figures from the original monument plan, is in a side chapel.

For views of the Colosseum stroll past the church and up the hill.

Above from far left:
Santa Pudenziana;
mosaic detail at
Palazzo Massimo;
steps link San Pietro in
Vincoli to Via Cavour.

Suburra

The legendary Suburra of Julius Caesar's day was an area with a dangerous reputation. Once home to gypsies, prostitutes, and thieves, it was popular with military troops looking for a night out.

Food and Drink 🍴

① DAGNINO
Galleria Esedra, Via Emanuele Orlando 75; tel: 06-481 8660; 7am–10.30pm; €
This classic 1950s-era café and pastry shop has a huge selection of Sicilian specialities like *cannoli* and *cassata* cakes. The smartly dressed waiters will also serve lunch and *arancine* (fried rice balls with cheese and various fillings).

② URBANA 47
Via Urbana 47; tel: 06-4788 4006; 10am–midnight; €–€€
A fun combination café, wine bar, restaurant with a contemporary atmosphere. Their wine selection is primarily from Lazio, and the cheese plate and salami plate are excellent.

③ LA CARBONARA
Via Panisperna 214; tel: 06-482 5176; 12.30–3pm, 7.30–11.30pm; €€€
This excellent trattoria is just out of the way enough to have great food and local atmosphere. The signature dish is, of course, pasta alla carbonara; their grilled meats are good too.

④ AI TRE SCALINI
Via Panisperna 251; tel: 06-489 07495; 12.30–11.30pm; €
This classic ivy-draped enoteca has been serving wines and simple dishes since 1895. Great relaxed atmosphere and excellent wines by the glass.

THE APPIAN WAY

Just outside the city centre is the verdant Via Appia Antica, a section of one of the most famous roads ever built. This original highway is lined with ancient tombs, ruins, sections of aqueduct and catacombs.

Rock Hard

The paving of a Roman road in the 3rd century BC was an immense undertaking. The roadbed was first levelled, and cushioned with mortar and small stones, then a layer of loose gravel was added. This was topped with interlocking basalt paving stones creating a flat surface. These stones fitted so well that it was nearly impossible to slip a knife blade between them. Ruts made by centuries of chariot traffic can still be seen.

DISTANCE 7km (4 miles)
TIME A full day
START Porta San Sebastiano
END Villa dei Quintili
POINTS TO NOTE
This child-friendly tour begins to the south of the city centre, and requires some form of transport either at the start or along its length *(see right)*. It is perfect for a picnic lunch and an afternoon's cycling to the various sights.

Right: Porta San Sebastiano.

Archeobus

There are a number of ways to get to the ancient gateway of the Porta San Sebastiano, where this route begins. Several city buses stop along the Via Appia Antica: the 118 from Via Aventino and the 218 from Piazza San Giovanni are the most direct lines. But by far the easiest choice is the municipal **Archeobus** (tel: 06-684 0901, www.trambusopen.com; 9am–5pm; charge; departure every 45 minutes). These bright green eco-friendly buses run a hop-on hop-off service between the Termini Train Station and most of the major sights along the Appian Way. Tickets for the Archeobus include a reduced entry rate for the catacombs of San Sebastiano, San Calisto and Domitilla. Tickets can be purchased in advance online, at Termini or onboard.

History

The *Via Appia Antica* (Old Appian Way) has been known for centuries as the 'Queen of Roads'. Sections of it have been used for more than 1,300 years for the transport of people and cargo in and out of the city. It is one of the finest achievements in military construction, running straight as an arrow for a total of 560 km (350 miles) to the Adriatic coast at the port of Brindisi.

The Via Appia originally ran from the Circus Maximus to Capua, and was built by the censor Appius Claudius Caecus in 312 BC. When the road was extended in 190 BC, to Brindisi, it became the gateway to the east. Eventually with the construction of the Baths of Caracalla *(see p.33)* and the Aurelian walls, the starting point was shifted to the Porta Appia (Porta San Sebastiano). The first section of this long road was lined with villas and the mausoleums of illustrious Romans. What we see now are small sections of this picturesque road *(see margin, left)*, connecting the ruins of a few of the ancient monuments.

quarters of the **Parco Regionale dell' Appia Antica** ❷ (Via Appia Antica 58; tel: 06-513 5316; www.parcoappia antica.it; 9.30am–5.30pm, to 4.30pm

Above from far left: Circus of Maxentius; section of aqueduct.

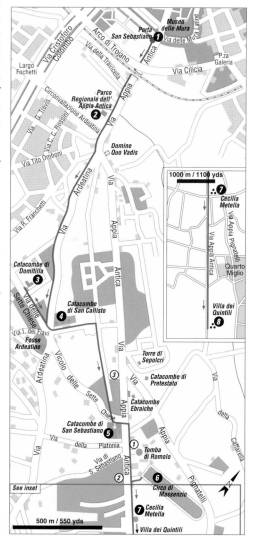

PORTA SAN SEBASTIANO

Start the tour at the ancient **Porta San Sebastiano** ❶, one of the few remaining gateways in the Aurelian wall. To the left of the gate is the entry to the **Museo delle Mura** (Museum of the Walls; tel: 06-7047 5284; Tue–Sun 9am–2pm; charge), a small museum with information about the construction of the Aurelian wall. Remains of the aqueducts and the surrounding fields are visible from the ramparts.

Visitors' Centre

Past the Porta San Sebastiano to the south is the first section of the Via Appia Antica. Here it is dusty and polluted from the endless stream of cars. Continue down the road for about 800m/yds (half a mile; or you could take the Archeobus to the next stop) to the Visitors' Centre and Park Head-

Domine Quo Vadis?
The church of Domine
Quo Vadis marks the
spot where in the 1st
century the Apostle
Peter was said to
have met Christ. The
astonished Peter said
to Christ 'Domine quo
vadis?' (Where are
you going Lord?), to
which he replied,
'I go to Rome to be
crucified a second
time'. Peter under-
stood this as a
personal message
and returned to face
his own martyrdom.

Below: the hop-on
hop-off Archeobus.

in winter). Their free map and
brochure lists about 50 different sites.
Consider hiring a bicycle for the day to
have access to all of the catacombs and
views of the oldest parts of the road.

Further along this stretch of busy
road, past the church of **Domine Quo
Vadis** *(see margin, left)* is a major fork.
Keep right to continue the walk on foot,
or take the Archeobus from the Parco
Regionale two stops to San Callisto.

VIA ARDEATINA

While much of the Via Appia Antica is
lined with tombs and monuments, it is
usually what lies below ground that is
most fascinating to visitors. Miles of
catacomb tunnels have been carved out
of the volcanic tufa. Over the centuries
many of the saints and early popes were
buried here, and they became shrines
and places of pilgrimage. Some of the
catacombs are open to the public with
guided or group entry only.

Catacombs of Domitilla

To continue on foot take the right fork
along the Via Ardeatina to the **Cata-**

combe di Domitilla ❸ (Via delle
Sette Chiese 282; tel: 06-511 0342;
www.catacombe.roma.it; Mon–Wed
9–noon, 2–5.30pm; charge). From the
San Callisto Archeobus stop, walk a
few minutes west, through the park,
from the Via Appia Antica to Via
Ardeatina. These are the largest network of catacombs in Rome. Most of
what is accessible was built between
the 1st and 2nd centuries, and by the
4th century it was used as a major
burial site for Christians. There are
some beautiful frescoes of both pagan
and Christian subjects.

Catacombs of San Callisto

Turning left at the Via delle Sette
Chiese, across the Via Ardeatina, is the
entrance to the **Catacombe di San Callisto** ❹ (Via Appia Antica 110; tel:
06-5130 1580; www.catacombe.roma.
it; Mon–Sun 8.30am–noon, 2.30–5pm;
charge), named after the first bishop
of Rome. San Callisto was the first official Christian burial area and it housed
the remains of many early popes.

VIA APPIA ANTICA

Continue south along the park area to
join the Via Appia Antica at the **Catacombe di San Sebastiano** ❺
(Catacombs of St Sebastian; Via
Appia Antica 136, tel: 06-785 0350;
www.catacombe.roma.it; Mon–Sat
8.30am–noon, 2.30–5.30pm; charge),
an extensive and popular catacomb
complex on four different levels.
Above is the 17th-century church to
the martyred St Sebastian.

Lunch Options

Across from the church are several good restaurants. The **Cecilia Metella** is popular, with good food and terrace views, see ⑪①. Nearby is the typical **Hostaria dell'Archeologia** or **Hostaria Antica Roma**, see ⑪② and ⑪③.

If you packed a picnic consider cycling or hopping on the Archeobus to the lovely Appia Pignatelli to sit under the remains of the aqueducts. From here continue the tour in reverse, backtracking north from the Villa dei Quintili to the Tomb of Cecilia Metella.

Circus of Maxentius

Refuelled from lunch, continue south to the **Circo di Massenzio** ❻ (Circus of Maxentius; Via Appia Antica 153; tel: 06-780 1324; Tue–Sat 9am–1pm; charge). This is the site of the magnificent stadium built by the Emperor Maxentius in 309. Both his villa and circus were constructed on the busy Via Appia to entertain sporting, military and businessmen on their way out of town.

Mausoleum of Cecilia Metella

Further along the Via Appia Antica is the mausoleum of **Cecilia Metella** ❼ (Via Appia Antica 161; tel: 06-780 2465; www.pierreci.it; 9am-4.30pm; charge). This circular family tomb was built around 50 BC and is one of the few grand monuments constructed for a woman. The building survives to this day because of Pope Boniface VIII Caetani, who gave the tomb to his relatives in the early 14th century. They remodelled and used it as a fortress to exact tolls on the Via Appia Antica. Cecilia

Metella is mentioned in Byron's epic poem *Childe Harold*.

Villa dei Quintili

The Via Appia Antica becomes much more rustic after this point, and it is here that you will find the tomb of Seneca and the eroded tomb of the famous Horatii. Further along are the remains of one of the largest country villas from the 2nd century. The **Villa dei Quintili** ❽ (Via Appia Nuova 1092; tel: 06-3996 7700; www.pierreci.it; 9am-4.30pm; charge) once belonged to the Quintili brothers who amassed great wealth as consuls. There is a shop, toilets and an Archeobus stop at the villa.

Food and Drink 🍴

① CECILIA METELLA

Via Appia Antica 125; tel: 06-513 6743; Tue–Sun; €€
This busy restaurant requires booking in the summer. It has a pleasant atmosphere and serves typical Italian dishes at good prices.

② HOSTARIA DELL' ARCHEOLOGIA

Via Appia Antica 139; tel: 06-788 0494; Wed–Mon; €€€
Popular with Italian tourists, the restaurant has a lovely garden and is known for its fish dishes with roasted potatoes, and a full selection of excellent wines.

③ HOSTARIA ANTICA ROMA

Via Appia Antica 87; tel: 06-513 2888; Tue–Sun; €€€
This large restaurant has plenty of indoor and garden seating. There is an old-style Roman atmosphere here, with a menu to match. They often have meats grilling.

Above from far left: mausoleum of Cecilia Metella; detail from the mausoleum; wandering the Appian Way; church of Saint Sebastian above the catacombs of the same name.

World War II Reminder
Along the Via Ardeatina is a sad memorial to Nazi atrocity. The Fosse Ardeatine (Via Ardeatina 174; tel: 06-513 6742; 8.30am–5pm; free) marks the spot where, on March 24, 1944, 335 Roman citizens were killed by firing squad. The people killed in the remote catacomb tunnels of Fosse Ardeatina were a group of randomly selected civilians, prisoners, and 73 Jews. The act was considered an exchange of life for 32 German soldiers who had been killed in a bomb attack. No one knew where the 335 innocent people had disappeared to until a local farmer spoke up about witnessing the scene. Today there is a mausoleum and memorial at the site.

Above from left: looking out over the gardens of Villa d'Este; Tivoli's Temple of Vesta; two views of the necropolis complex at Cerveteri.

LUNCH IN TIVOLI

From Piazza Garibaldi, a 10-minute walk east towards the river will take you to restaurant and former Roman bath house **Antiche Terme di Diana**, see ⅊①, a good lunch option. Alternatively, try trattoria **Gallo d'Oro**, see ⅊②.

Before heading to Villa d'Este, stroll along Via della Sibilla (in the north-eastern corner of town) where you'll see the round Republican-era **Tempio di Vesta** and the rectangular **Tempio della Sibilla**, dating from 2 AD.

VILLA D'ESTE

Zigzag your way through the medieval streets back towards Piazza Garibaldi and head north on Via Boselli until you reach **Villa d'Este** ❷ (Piazza Trento, tel: 07-7431 2070; Tue–Sun 8.30am–1hr before dusk; charge). The park surrounding the Baroque villa was elected Best European Garden of 2007.

The surrounding gardens are laid out, in typical Italian style, on four sweeping terraces, the first of which offers soul-stirring views. Head down to the second level for **Diana's Grotto** and the **Fontana del Bicchierone** (Fountain of the Great Cup) by Bernini. Go down the staircase on the left for the intricate **Fontana della Rometta**, a miniature representation of Rome landmarks, and, from here, walk behind the **Nymphaeum** (Corridor of the Nymphs) cascade. This brings you to the **Viale delle Cento Fontane** (Avenue of a Hundred Fountains), a row of pipes that spray water into the air, and the impressive **Fontana dell'Ovato** (Oval Fountain), decorated with nymphs.

Further down still is the central **Fontana dei Draghi** (Fountain of the Dragons), made in honour of Pope Gregory XIII, who was once a guest here, and whose papal insignia included a dragon, and, finally, the 400-year-old **Fontana dell'Organo Idraulico**, with an elaborate water-operated organ that still works.

Fountain Feat
Water is diverted from the Aniene river for the Villa d'Este's some 500 fountains; it is a feat of hydraulics ingenious by today's standards, let alone those of the 16th century.

Villa Gregoriana

Near Tivoli's Temple of Vesta is the entrance to Parco di Villa Gregoriana (Piazza Tempio di Vesta; tel 06-3996 7701; www.villagregoriana.it; Apr–Oct 10am–6.30pm, Mar and Nov Tue–Sun 10am–2.30pm, Dec–Feb by appointment only; charge). The gardens were commissioned by Pope Gregory in 1826 following flooding of the Aniene river. To avert future floods the Papal government diverted the river's course, which resulted in a breathtaking 120-m- (400-ft-) high waterfall in the hills. The former riverbed left grottoes and rock formations, which, together with the cascade, provide a lovely backdrop for the Temple of Vesta and other archaeological finds.

Food and Drink 🍴

① ANTICHE TERME DI DIANA
6 Via dei Sosii; tel 07-7433 5239; Tue–Sun lunch and dinner; €€
Housed in an ancient Roman thermal structure, this elegant restaurant serves authentic Tiburtine cuisine. Try the giant ravioli with black truffle. Outdoor area, too.

② GALLO D'ORO
Via del Duomo 53; tel 07-7433 5363; Wed–Mon lunch and dinner; €
A popular trattoria and pizzeria serving Roman dishes. Near the cathedral.

CERVETERI

This tour is a blend of the best that the Roman countryside has to offer: Unesco-protected Etruscan ruins over kilometres of lush countryside, and vineyards where you can sample Lazio's up-and-coming wines.

The well-preserved ruins of the once-powerful Etruscans are scattered throughout the regions of Lazio and Tuscany, where they settled *c*.800 BC. Although the origins of the Etruscans continue to puzzle scholars, they were undoubtedly a highly civilised people with a hearty appetite for life. Hundreds of Etruscan tombs have survived, many with wall paintings depicting dancing, music-making, hunting and fighting.

CERVETERI

Cerveteri is home to the Banditaccia necropolis complex, a Unesco World Heritage Site that provides a comprehensive insight into Etruscan life. In the 7th and 6th centuries BC, the settlement, called Kysry, was one of the most powerful cities in Etruria, with a population of around 25,000. Eventually, however, the barbaric strength of Rome wiped away what had been a joyous and refined civilisation. The town became Caere, now Cerveteri.

Cerveteri National Museum

A good place to start your tour is Cerveteri's **Museo Nazionale Cerite** (Piazza Santa Maria; tel: 06-994 1354; Tue–Sun 8.30am–7.30pm; free), located inside a 13th-century castle. Much of the art from the

DISTANCE Cerveteri is 43km (27 miles) northwest of Rome
TIME A full day
START Cerveteri
END Casale Cento Corvi winery
POINTS TO NOTE

Trains run from Termini station to Cerveteri-Ladispoli, where local buses run to Cerveteri and the necropolis.

COTRAL buses leave from Cornelia (metro line A). It's a 25-minute walk to the necropolis, or a local bus ride.

By car, take Via Aurelia (SS1) or autostrada A12 Roma-Civitavecchia and exit at Cerveteri (40km).

The Etruscan sites close on Monday. Bring a torch to illuminate the tombs.

Staying Overnight

If you plan see all three Etruscan sites mentioned in this tour, you will most likely need to plan an overnight trip. Montalto di Castro near Vulci is an ideal base. Check out Hotel Vulci (Via Aurelia Km 111; tel: 07-668 9402; www.hotelvulci.it) 5km (3 miles) from Vulci, or the more modern, beachfront Hotel Enterprise (32 Via delle Tamerici; tel: 07-6680 2145/6).

Train Tour

There's an eco-friendly electric train for guided tours around the Banditaccia necropolis, if you don't want to walk the whole thing. The timetable varies according to the season; log on to www.glietruschivisti daltreno.it for details.

Below: crushing grapes in the traditional way.

town's heyday is now held in Rome itself, but there are still notable examples of pottery and sarcophagi in this little museum.

THE NECROPOLIS

Close to the museum is Piazza Aldo Moro, the town's main square. From here, catch bus G or walk for around 25 minutes (head downhill, turn right into the Via del Sasso, and follow the signs) to reach the **Banditaccia Necropolis ❶** (entrance off Via del Sasso; tel: 06-994 0001; www.ticket eria.it; Tue–Sun 8.30am–dusk; charge). It contains thousands of tombs and cinerary sites made of great mounds of earth *(tumoli)* with carved stone bases, all of which are laid out like a city,

branching off the Via dei Inferi (Road of the Dead). No two tombs are alike.

The burial grounds open to the public stretch for over 2km (1¼ miles), and contain some 2,000 tombs, the oldest of which date back to the 8th century BC; the more elaborate ones are painted and frescoed. The names of the family members buried within are inscribed throughout, in a remarkably efficient manner. There are said to be almost 40,000 tombs in the surrounding area, many still undiscovered.

Highlights

Once inside, you will be given a map and guide, and allowed to roam freely. The most notable tombs are labelled clearly in Italian and English, and generally describe the family buried

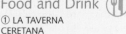

Food and Drink

① LA TAVERNA CERETANA
Via Ceretana 29; tel: 06-994 1589; Tue–Sun lunch and dinner; €
A classic taverna with lots of Etruscan charm. The back room has a quirky grotto-like ceiling. Italian and Roman specialities are fresh and reasonably priced. Try the gnocchi alla taverna: potato dumplings with a tomato and bacon sauce, peas and pesto.

② ANTICA LOCANDA LE GINESTRE
Piazza Santa Maria 5; tel: 06-994 0672; www.le-ginestre.it; Tue–Sun lunch and dinner; €€–€€€
Sophisticated Italian cuisine with excellent sommelier service and extensive wine list. Ask for a table with a view of the necropolis. A lunch to linger over.

inside or the elements that render the tomb unique. Bring a torch to get a better view.

Keep an eye out for the following: the 6th-century BC **Tomba dei Capitelli**, a fine example of the elegant Etruscan architectural style, with visible ceiling beams and ornately carved Corinthian columns; the remarkable **Tomba dei Rilievi** or 'Tomba Bella', one of the few tombs encased in glass – it contains colourful painted reliefs dating to 4 BC and its wall decorations depict everyday household items and even the family pets; and the **Tomba della Colonna Dorica**, with a central Doric column and remnants of various other columns.

Lunch Stop

After touring the Necropolis, head back to Cerveteri for lunch. Most restaurants serve until around 3pm. Just off the main square, **La Taverna Ceretana**, see ①①, is decorated like an Etruscan grotto, and serves simple Italian fare; across from the museum is the upscale **Antica Locanda Le Ginestre**, see ①②.

LAZIO VINEYARD

Some of the best white wine in Lazio comes from Cerveteri, where the tuff-rock soil bestows a rich mineral bouquet. After lunch, head back to the main piazza (where the COTRAL buses stop) for local (orange) bus A. Buses run to and from Cerveteri throughout the day, stopping directly in front of the winery. If you're in the car, head back to Via Aurelia, and head north.

Wine Tour

The wine producers of **Casale Cento Corvi** ❷ (Via Aurelia Km 45,500; tel: 06-990 3902; email: azienda@casale centocorvi.it; Mon–Sat 8.30am–12.30pm, 3–7pm, Sun 9.30am–12.30pm) are making waves and winning awards for a red wine made from the Giacchè grape, thought to have died out centuries ago.

Generations of wine-making, combined with the latest technology, have brought Giacchè back to life, first in a laboratory, then in dry and dessert versions. To visit the winery and sample the whole range (the whites are delicious too, and labels are inspired by Etruscan relics and legends), call or email in advance of your visit.

Above from far left: entrance to a tomb; wine barrels; Tarquinia Museum.

The Etruscan Trail

If travelling by car, you could also visit Tarquinia ❸ and Vulci ❹. The beautiful medieval walled city of Tarquinia sits high upon clifftops and is home to another Unesco-protected necropolis, Monterozzi (tel: 07-6685 6308; Tue–Sun 8.30am–2pm in winter, Tue–Sun 8.30am–dusk in summer; charge). First, visit the Museo Nazionale Tarquinense (Piazza Cavour; tel: 07-6685 6036; Tue–Sun 8.30am–7.30pm; charge), where highlights include an elaborate life-sized relief of a pair of winged horses, gold jewellery, vases, sarcophagi and beautiful frescoes. At Vulci a magnificent former abbey-turned-castle looms over the remains of an ancient Roman-Etruscan city, housing the Museo Nazionale Archeologico di Vulci (tel: 07-6143 7787; Tue–Sat 9am–6pm; charge). Vulci is surrounded by four separate necropolis sites, all contained within the Parco Naturalistico Archeologico Vulci (tel: 07-6687 9729; call to organise a visit 48 hours in advance, or turn up on Sun at 3pm; charge).

CASTELLI ROMANI

Under an hour's drive southeast of Rome will transport you to medieval villages, verdant gardens, the Pope's summer residence and a pagan shrine to the goddess Diana. There's plenty to eat and drink along the way, so take your time and bring your appetite.

DISTANCE Frascati is 21km (13 miles) southeast of Rome

TIME At least a full day

START Frascati

END Nemi

POINTS TO NOTE

This tour requires a car, but all towns mentioned are accessible by train (www.trenitalia.it) or COTRAL bus services, which depart from the car park at Anagnina station at the end of metro line A.

Overnight Option

If you wish to extend your trip overnight, try the bed and breakfast Vigna del Sole (Via Antonio Vivaldi 9; tel: 06-938 4342; www.vignedelsole.it). Full of country charm, it is just 10 minutes from Marino.

In the Alban Hills southeast of Rome, the 13 towns known as the Castelli Romani all grew up around feudal castles and have seen the coming and going of Rome's rich and powerful retreating from the urban chaos. Today they are renowned for their excellent food and wine, and local character.

Getting There

This route covers Frascati, Castel Gandolfo and Nemi, with optional stops in Marino and Genzano. To get to Frascati, take the Tuscolana exit from the GRA ring road onto road no. 215, and look out for signs to the town.

The proximity of the towns allows for much flexibility. If you plan to see the Papal Palace in the morning, drive straight through Frascati and head to Castel Gandolfo as your first stop.

FRASCATI

The nearest, and most famous, of the Castelli, **Frascati ❶** is home to countless villas and gardens, a namesake wine and a breathtaking panorama of Rome.

Start the day with a cappuccino in one of the cafés off **Piazza Roma**. Cruise the bread and cheese shops and market square at **Via Regina Margherita** (around a 15-minute walk

through the winding medieval streets) and perhaps pack a picnic for later.

Villa Aldobrandini

Walk or drive 1.5km (1 mile) southeast of town to **Villa Aldobrandini** (Via GG Massaia; tel: 06-942 0331; 9am–1pm, 3–6pm, till 5pm in winter; free, *see margin, right*). This stately, ornate 17th-century Baroque villa is still occupied by the Aldobrandini family, but you can visit the gloriously tended gardens, complete with fountains. The terraced facade overlooks the city and the view is perhaps the best panorama in Lazio: it is affectionately known as La Terraza su Roma (the terrace of Rome). Between the villa and the hill rising behind it is the **Teatro delle Acque** fountain by Carlo Maderno.

If you fancy lunch at this point, try **Cacciani**, see 🍴① (just off Piazza Roma back in Frascati).

On leaving, take the SS218 towards Castel Gandolfo, which becomes the SS216; Marino is a turn off to the right.

MARINO

Also known as la Città del Vino, or the city of wine, **Marino ❷** gives Frascati wine a run for its money, especially in early autumn. On the first Sunday of October, it hosts the Sagra del Uva, a celebration of the grape harvest and a whole-hearted tribute to Bacchus. For about an hour the fountain at **Piazza Matteotti** spouts wine instead of water, as thirsty hordes fill their glasses.

For lunch try a porchetta sandwich from the **Mangia e Bere** stand, see

🍴②, in Piazza Lepanto (the other end of Corso Trieste from Piazza Matteotti).

Directly across Corso Trieste stands the pretty Baroque **Basilica San Barnaba** (Piazza San Barnaba), which houses several notable works of art, among them the *Martyrdom of St Bartholomew* by Guercino.

CASTEL GANDOLFO

When arriving from the north (from Frascati or Marino), take the SS216 (Via Bruno Buozzi) for **Castel Gandolfo ❸**. In keeping with 400 years of tradition, the Pope spends his summers here at a luxurious palace overlooking **Lago Albano**. The lake is a popular spot for boating and swimming, and there's a pleasant calm breeze.

Take Via Palazzo Pontificio to reach the **Residenza Papale**, which was designed by Bernini. The palace interior can only be visited with special

Above from far left: Papal Palace at Castel Gandolfo; a flask of Frascati in a backstreet cantina; Villa Aldobrandini.

Bring Your Own
It's common practice throughout the Castelli to bring your own food to wine shops, pay for a glass or a carafe and eat on the premises.

Villa Aldobrandini
Stop at Frascati's tourist office (Piazza Marconi, 1; tel: 06-942 0331; Mon–Fri 9am–1pm, 3–5pm) to procure a pass to Villa Aldobrandini. You don't need to reserve in advance, but you do have to have a pass.

Food and Drink 🍴

① CACCIANI
Via A. Diaz, Frascati; tel: 06-942 9378; Tue–Sun lunch and dinner; €€–€€€
The hotel restaurant offers gorgeous views from its terrace seating and a menu of creative takes on the regional culinary canons. Try the fusilli with broccoli, mint, pecorino and pancetta. Reservations recommended.

② MANGIA E BERE
Piazza Lepanto, Marino; tel: 06-936 7134; €
Buy a herb-roasted suckling pig sandwich and a glass of wine to take away, or sit at the table in front.

Above from left:
Nemi; theatre at
Ostia Antica.

Rocca di Papa
The town of Rocca
di Papa (The Pope's
Rock; *below*) lies
a few kilometres east
of Marino, on the
northern flank of the
Monte Cavo, the
highest peak of the
Alban Hills (949m/
3,114ft). This attract-
ive medieval town
has a *quartiere
bavarese*, named
after the Bavarian
mercenaries who
were stationed here
by Emperor Ludwig III
in the 1320s.

permission, but is still a sight to behold.
Catch the Sunday Angelus in the
Piazza della Libertà, near the entrance
to the palace, at noon in summer. The
Wednesday papal audience generally
starts around 10am and requires a
reservation (tel: 06-6982).

GENZANO

If you're travelling in early to mid-
June, stop at the medieval town of
Genzano ❹ (along the SS7) for its
annual *infiorata* (flower festival; www.
infiorata.it). For one three-day weekend, residents and guest artists adorn
Via Livia (leading from central Piazza
IV Novembre to the church of Santa
Maria della Cima) with enormous
mosaics made of flower petals and
stems. The work requires 500 tons of
flowers. At the close of the Sunday,
the town's children scamper through
the street en masse.

NEMI

If coming from Frascati or Castel Gandolfo, take **Via dei Laghi** up and around
Lago Albano; it is a gorgeous drive.
From Genzano you'll head round the
southeastern edge of Lago di Nemi on
curvy local roads for 4km (2½ miles).

The most peaceful of the Castelli villages, in pre-Christian times **Nemi** ❺
was the site of an ancient shrine to
Diana, goddess of the hunt, and one of
Rome's most vociferous cults. Ruins of
the ancient temple can be seen on the
slopes between the village and the lake.

Evidence of enthusiastic pagan worship was also discovered at the depths
of the lake, where Emperor Caligula
constructed immense barges for
floating ceremonies to the Egyptian
goddess Isis. They were first discovered
during the Renaissance, but not fully
recovered until the 1930s, under Mussolini. The lake was drained, and two
ships measuring more than 70m
(200ft) long and 20m (65ft) wide were
revealed; they were, however, destroyed
towards the end of World War II.

Replicas were put in the lakeside
Museo delle Navi Romane di Nemi
(Via del Tempio di Diana 15; tel: 07-
7363 3935; Mon–Sat 9am–1.30pm,
2.30–6pm, till 5pm in winter; charge).
The museum is 3km (2 miles) from
the village of Nemi. Take Corso Vittorio Emanuele to Via Garibaldi; a
right turn on to Via Plebiscito will
bring you to Via del Tempio di Diana.

To return to Rome, rejoin the SS7
(Via Appia) and head back to the GRA
or follow the blue road signs for 'Roma'.

OSTIA ANTICA

Long overshadowed by the ruins of the resort-town of Pompeii, the port city of Ostia Antica is an easy daytrip from Rome and provides a marvellous picture of ancient Roman life. A 30-minute train ride gets you there, and the nearby beach allows for some leisure time after exploring.

OSTIA ANTICA

Ostia Antica (717 Viale dei Romagnoli; tel: 06-5635 8099; www.ostiantica.info/www.ostia-antica.org; Tue–Sun 8.30am–7pm, till 5.30pm in winter; charge) is not only one of the best preserved of all ancient Roman cities, but it also offers a look at varying periods and styles of Roman city life.

The earliest town wall went up in 335 BC, with the sea protecting the settlement at the western side. After nearly 600 years as a bustling port city, Ostia saw a decline during the 4th century AD, suffered a Barbarian sacking 100 years later and was slowly buried under silt and sand, forgotten for centuries.

Sitting at the mouth of the Tiber, Ostia was the first landing point for all the treasures bound for Rome from the far-flung corners of the empire. The shipping business was especially lucrative, and remnants of several luxurious homes are visible at the archaeological site. Maps are available for sale, and, given how much there is to see, it's recommended that you buy one.

Decumanus Maximus

Enter the park, pass under the **Porta Romana** city gates and head down the main street, **Decumanus Maximus**,

DISTANCE Ostia Antica is 25km (15 miles) southwest of Rome
TIME A full day
START Ostia Antica
END Lido di Ostia
POINTS TO NOTE

Trains depart daily from Piramide (metro line B). Alight at Ostia Antica – the ruins are just across the highway bridge. After Ostia Antica take the train back to Rome (direction: Porta San Paolo), or continue to the beaches and restaurants at Lido di Ostia Centro and the next few stops.

Ostia Antica is closed on Mondays.

Transport Tip
Purchase the one-day *(giornaliero)* pass for €4. It's valid until midnight, and allows unlimited rides on the metro, buses and Roma–Ostia train line.

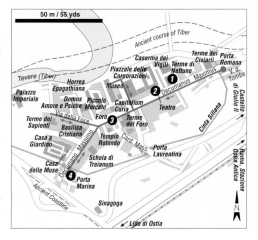

which once connected Ostia to Rome. To your right are the **Terme dei Cisiarii** (Baths of the Coachmen), named after a mosaic depicting mule-drawn carriages.

Baths of Neptune

Stay on the main road and you will pass the foundations of shops and offices. Look for ancient tavern counters and the remains of a bakery's stone ovens; a mosaic of a fish indicates what was sold in one store. Further ahead on the right is a large bath complex, the **Terme di Nettuno ❶** (Baths of Neptune), just behind a row of shops. Elaborate mosaics depict Neptune and his wife

Below: detail of a well-preserved mosaic in the Baths of Neptune.

Amphitrite among sea creatures. The series of rooms contains many more mosaics, and a large *palestra*, the precursor to a modern weight-lifting gym. Working out was presumably a real pleasure among the grand marble-columned portico surrounding it.

Behind the baths are the walls of the fire station, **Caserma dei Vigili**. The use of oil lamps by night in the old town here created quite a fire hazard. The fire fighters, or *vigilis*, also policed the city, much like modern Italy's traffic *vigili*.

Back near the main road, there are remnants of an inscription that once read: FORTVNATVS VINUM E CRATERA QVOD SITIS BIBE or 'Fortunus says to drink wine from the vessel because you are thirsty.'

Theatre

Next you will encounter the large and virtually intact **Teatro ❷** (theatre), with 3,000 seats. Constructed under Agrippa, during the 1st century BC, it was enlarged a century later. The orchestra was originally covered in marble and was flooded for small-scale sea scenes. Keep an eye out for small shrines; many Christians were executed in the theatre.

Behind the theatre, the big shippers and traders had their offices in the **Piazzale delle Corporazioni** (Square of the Guilds). There were at least 60 of these offices, and it's worth seeing their ancient 'trademarks' and the mosaics depicting scenes of busy city life. The River Tiber ran right by the piazza in those days (it has since slightly changed its course).

Forum

Continuing on the main road, on the left is the former laundry service. Turn right for the excavation **museum**, bar and bathrooms, otherwise continue straight ahead and take the road for the **Capitolium Curia**, which stands at one end of the **Foro** ❸ (Forum). This temple to the Capitoline triad (Jupiter, Juna and Minerva) has steps as impressive as those in any modern capital city.

On the other side of the forum is the **Tempio Rotondo**, round – like the Pantheon – and dedicated to deified emperors. Less distinguishable are the remains of a courthouse *(curia)*, city council and a basilica. Further along is a round temple, dedicated to the deified emperors of Rome.

After you exit the forum you will reach a fork. **Decumano Massimo** veers slightly left toward the **Porta Marina** ❹, the ancient coastline, where a synagogue dating back to the 1st century BC was recently uncovered. You'll pass an expansive house and garden structure in Hadrianesque grandeur.

Return to the fork. **Via della Foce** veers right toward **Domus Amore e Psiche**, named after a statue of Cupid and Psyche found on the premises. Marble and granite columns support pretty arches, and there's a tiny courtyard beyond. Further up the street are more bathhouses and a granary.

MEDIEVAL CASTLE

On your way back to the train station, turn down **Piazzale della Rocca** from Viale dei Romagnoli, and you will see the **Castello di Giulio II**, built in 1483 by Baccio Pontelli and regarded as one of the best examples of Renaissance fortification; also here is the medieval town of Ostia. The castle was constructed as a papal apartment and is now a small museum. The frescoes on the main staircase are by Baldassare Peruzzi. Phone ahead to organise a visit to the castle (tel: 06-5635 8024).

LIDO DI OSTIA

If you plan on soaking up some sun before dinner, reserve a table in advance at **La Vecchia Pineta**, see ⑪①, and take the train to **Castel Fusano**. The beach club and restaurant are directly in front of you. Lounge chairs and umbrellas are available for rent. Sandwiches and ice creams are available at the bar on site.

Another option is to get off at the previous stops of **Ostia Centro** or **Stella Polare**, and head to the beachfront avenue where you can grab a slice of pizza. This area is packed with beach clubs, many of which are free.

Remember that trains back to Rome stop running at 10.20pm.

Below: evocative ruins at Ostia Antica.

Food and Drink 🍴

① LA VECCHIA PINETA
4 Via Acquilone; tel: 06-5647 0282; Mon–Sat lunch and dinner; €–€€
An attractive glassed-in seafront location adds to the appeal of this seafood restaurant. Try *spaghetti allo scoglio*, a spicy clam sauce, and fried *(fritto misto)* or grilled *(grigliata mista)* mixed seafood platters.

DIRECTORY

A user-friendly alphabetical listing of practical information, plus hand-picked hotels and restaurants, clearly organised by area, to suit all budgets and tastes.

A

ADMISSION FEES

Museum admission fees vary, but the major ones range from €7–12 while the minor ones cost about €4. Most state or municipal museums offer free entrance to EU citizens under 18 or over 65. The entrance ticket to the Palatine can be used to visit the Colosseum. Entrance to the Roman Forum, the Pantheon and all basilicas and churches is free, as is entrance to the Vatican Museums on the last Sunday of the month (expect long queues).

B

BUSINESS HOURS

In general shops open Mon 3.30–7.30pm, Tues–Sat 9am–1pm and 3.30–7.30pm. Many shops and restaurants close for two weeks in August. Churches generally open 7am–7pm with a three-hour lunch break (times vary). Banks open Mon–Fri 8.30am–1.30pm and 2.45–4pm; a few in the city centre also open Saturday morning. State and city museums are closed on Monday, but there are a few exceptions: the Colosseum, the Roman Forum and the Vatican Museums.

C

CHILDREN

Little ones are welcome everywhere. Villa Borghese Park offers plenty of outdoor entertainment, with paddleboats, bike rentals, and expansive green space. The Zoo is located on the grounds *(see p.56)*, and there's a puppet theatre in the Pincio Gardens *(see p.57)*.

Nearby, the Explora Children's Museum is packed with interactive exhibits and kid-size dioramas, all aimed to teach and entertain *(see p.19)*.

CLIMATE

Despite some very unusual weather in the past few years (snow and hail in July, heatwaves in May), Rome can still be said to have a classic Mediterranean climate: mild winters and very hot, long summers. July and August are the hottest and most humid months, and late-August rain showers are becoming the norm.

April, May, September and October are the best months to visit as the weather is usually sunny and warm.

CLOTHING

Light summer clothes are suitable from spring to autumn. The Roman heat is sometimes alleviated by a sea breeze by day and evenings can be cool, even in summer, so keep a jacket on hand. Hats and sunglasses are recommended for sun protection.

Rainfall is rare in mid-summer, but when the deluge does come, it's often a surprise afternoon shower that rarely lasts for long. November and early December are notoriously rainy, so bring your raincoat. In winter, you'll want to dress in layers.

CRIME

The main problem tourists experience in Rome is petty crime: pick-pocketing and bag snatching, together with theft from parked cars. Leave money and valuables in the hotel safe, and keep an eye on your handbag. Be especially vigilant on packed buses.

Report a theft *(furto)* to the police as soon as possible: you will need the police report for any insurance claim and to replace stolen documents. For information on the nearest police station call the Questura Centrale, 15 Via San Vitale, tel: 06-468 611 or ask for the *questura più vicino*.

CUSTOMS

Visitors from EU countries are not obliged to declare goods imported into or exported from Italy if they are for personal use, up to the following limits: 800 cigarettes, 200 cigars or 1 kg of tobacco; 10 litres of spirits (over 22 percent alcohol) or 20 litres of fortified wine (under 22 percent alcohol).

For US citizens, the duty-free allowance is 200 cigarettes, 50 cigars; 1 litre of spirits or 2 litres of wine; one 50 g bottle of perfume and duty-free gifts to the value of US$ 200–800 depending on how often you travel.

D

DISABLED TRAVELLERS

Rome is a difficult city for people with disabilities. However, things are improving, and the following attractions have installed ramps and lifts: the Vatican Museums, Galleria Doria Pamphilj, Castel Sant'Angelo, Palazzo Venezia, St Peter's and Galleria Borghese.

For information on disabled access, contact Roma Per Tutti (tel: 06-5717 7094/ 800-810 810, www.roma per-tutti.it). Trambus (tel: 06-4695 4001; www.trambus.com) also offers a pick-up service for tourists with disabilities. Reserve before 1pm and confirm by 6pm the day before. Each ride costs €23 and is payable in cash.

E

ELECTRICITY

Standard is 220 volts AC, 50 cycles. Sockets have either two or three round pins. For UK visitors, adaptors can be bought before you leave home, or at airports and stations. Travellers from the US will need a transformer.

EMBASSIES/CONSULATES

If your passport is lost or stolen you will need to obtain a police report *(see under Crime)* and have proof of your identity to get a new one.

Australia: 5 Via Antonio Bosio; tel: 06-852 721; www.italy.embassy.gov.au

Canada: 30 Via Zara; tel: 06-854 441; www.canada.it

Ireland: 3 Piazza Campitelli; tel: 06-697 9121; www.ambasciata-irlanda.it

New Zealand: 28 Via Zara; tel: 06-441 7171; www.nzembassy.com

South Africa: 14 Via Tanaro; tel: 06-852 541; www.sudafrica.it
UK: 80a Via XX Settembre; tel: 06-4220 0001; www.britain.it
US: 119A Via Veneto; tel: 06-46741; www.usembassy.it

EMERGENCY NUMBERS

Police 113, Carabinieri 112, Fire 115, Ambulance 118.

G

GAY TRAVELLERS

Slowly but surely, the capital is inching its way toward becoming a more tolerant and gay-friendly city. A number of bars, restaurants and clubs have opened up within the city centre, and welcome a mixed crowd, no longer banishing homosexuality to the far edges and dark corners of the city.

Arcigay Roma, 35B Via Goito; tel: 06-6450 1102; www.arcigayroma.it; Thur (Welcome Night) 7–9pm, Fri (Living Room) 6–9pm; metro and bus: Termini. This branch of the Italian Arcigay association serves as a meeting and information point, and a centre for social activism. Many clubs require an Arcigay membership card, which can be purchased on site.

Circolo Mario Mieli di Cultura Omosessuale, 2A Via Efeso; tel: 06-541 3985; www.mariomieli.org; Mon–Fri 10am–6pm; metro: San Paolo, bus: 23. Rome's most respected gay, lesbian and transgender organisation serves as a cultural and counselling centre; its website is a viable resource for all things gay in the city.

H

HEALTH

EU residents are entitled to the same medical treatment as an Italian citizen. Visitors will need to obtain an EHIC card *(see* www.ehic.org.uk *for information)* before they go.

US citizens are advised to take out private health insurance. Canadian citizens are covered by a reciprocal arrangement between the Italian and Canadian governments.

Chemists

Chemists *(farmacie)* can easily be identified by their sign with a green cross on it. Farmacia della Stazione, 51 Piazza dei Cinquecento (corner of Via Cavour), tel: 06-488 0019, and Farmacia Piram Omeopatia, 228 Via Nazionale, tel: 06-488 0754, are open 24 hours.

Emergencies

If you need emergency treatment, call 118 for an ambulance or to get information on the nearest hospital with an emergency department *(pronto soccorso)*.

Hospitals

The most central hospital is Ospedale Fatebenefratelli, Isola Tiberina, tel: 06-68371. If your child is sick, Ospedale Paediatric Bambino Gesù (4 Piazza Sant'Onofrio, tel: 06-68591) is a highly regarded paediatric hospital.

I

INTERNET

Many of the city's green spaces are now wireless hotspots; you can surf the internet free in villas Borghese, Pamphilj, Ada and Torlonia (*see also* www. romawireless.com).

There is no shortage of internet cafés in Rome:

Easy Everything, 2 Via Barberini; tel: 06-4290 3388; www.easyeverything. com; daily 8am–2am. Some of the cheapest rates in town.

The Netgate, 25 Piazza Firenze; tel: 06-687 9098; Mon–Sat 7am–9pm. Trained staff and plenty of hi-tech computers near Piazza di Spagna.

A popular hangout for students abroad, **Good** (8/9 Via di S. Dorotea; tel: 06-9727 7979) doubles as a wireless hotspot and café. A smattering of tables outside allows for good people-watching in Trastevere.

L

LANGUAGE

You will not find English spoken everywhere in Rome, as you do in some other European cities. However, Italians are usually helpful and quick to understand what you want. Italians appreciate foreigners making an effort to speak their language, even if it's only a few words. In the major hotels and shops, staff usually speak some English. For a list of Italian vocabulary, see the pull-out map that accompanies this guide.

LOST PROPERTY

For property lost on trains anywhere in Rome ask at the Termini Station's left-luggage office, located at the underground level (-1) near platform 24, open from 6am–midnight.

For property lost on public transport (except trains) contact the bus and tram network (Atac) lost property office: 06-6769 3214; www.atac. roma.it; Mon, Fri 8.30am–1pm; Tues–Thurs 3–5pm.

M

MAPS

Free city maps are available from the tourist offices *(see p.108)*. Transport maps can be downloaded from the Atac website (www.atac.roma.it) while more detailed transport maps (called Roma MetroBus) can be bought at any newsstand in the centre.

MEDIA

Newspapers and Magazines
Most important European dailies are available on the day of publication from street kiosks in the city centre, as is the *International Herald Tribune*.

The main Rome-based Italian newspapers are *La Repubblica* and *Il Messaggero*. Other Italian newspapers such as *Il Corriere della Sera* publish Rome editions with local news and entertainment listings. The best weekly guide in Rome is *Roma C'è*, with comprehensive listings on every-

Above from far left: national flags outside the monument of Il Vittoriano; gay friendly bar; Isola Tiberina is home to the city's most central hospital; traffic warden on Piazza Venezia.

Left Luggage
You can leave your luggage at Termini station for a daily fee per bag. Fiumicino Airport also has 24-hour left-luggage facilities in the international terminals.

thing from museums and exhibitions to shopping, eating, films and festivals. It comes out on Wednesday and is available from any newsstand. Listings are in Italian, but there is an abbreviated section in English.

Wanted in Rome (www.wantedinrome.com), a fortnightly magazine in English, is another good source of listings information.

The American Magazine (www.theamericanmag.com) is a monthly magazine on Italian cultural life, available from newsstands in the centre.

MONEY

The unit of currency in Italy is the euro (€), which is divided into 100 cents. There are €5, 10, 20, 50, 100, 200 and 500 notes, coins worth €1 and €2, and 1, 2, 5, 10, 20 and 50 cent coins.

Changing Money

You need your passport or identification card when changing money, which can be a slow operation. Not all banks will provide cash against a credit card, and some may refuse to cash travellers' cheques in certain currencies. On the whole, the larger banks (those with a national or international network) will be the best for tourist transactions.

Travellers' cheques are the safest way to carry money around, but not the most economical, since banks charge a commission for cashing them, and shops and restaurants give unfavourable exchange rates if they accept them at all.

Credit and Debit Cards

While major credit cards are accepted by most hotels, shops and restaurants, it's best to keep some cash on hand, as the card-reading machines are frequently out of order.

Cash machines (ATMs), called Bancomat, can be found throughout central Rome, and are the easiest and generally the cheapest way of obtaining cash.

Tipping

Service is not included in a restaurant bill unless noted on the menu as *servizio*. It is customary to leave a modest tip, but nothing like the 10–15 percent common in other countries. Romans usually leave between €1–5, depending on how satisfied they were with the service; tourists are expected to be slightly more generous.

When you take a taxi, just round the fare up to the nearest euro.

P

POST

Post offices are open Mon–Fri 8.30am– 1pm; central post offices are generally open in the afternoon, too.

Stamps *(francobolli)* can be bought at many tobacconists *(tabacchi)*. Italian postboxes are red or yellow, but blue boxes specifically for foreign letters have been set up in the centre. Postboxes have two slots, *per la città* (for Rome) and *tutte le altre destinazioni* (everywhere else). For fast delivery (up to three days in Europe and five to the

Cover Charge
By law, the old cover charge, called *pane e coperto* (bread and table linen), has been abolished, but still appears on many menus. Keep an eye out: in many cases it has turned into a charge for bread, which you may refuse if you wish.

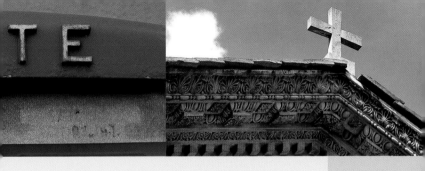

rest of the world), ask for *posta priori-taria* (priority post) stamps.

The main post office is in Piazza San Silvestro, just off Via del Corso (Mon–Sat 8am–7pm). The post office at the train station is also open all day Mon–Sat.

PUBLIC HOLIDAYS

1 January New Year's Day
6 January Epiphany
Easter Monday
25 April Liberation Day
1 May May Day
Whit Sunday (Monday not a holiday)
15 August The Assumption of Mary
1 November All Saints' Day
8 December Immaculate Conception
25–26 December Christmas and St Stephen's Day.

Holidays and Festivals

New Year's Eve is very big business in Rome: drinking, dancing, noisy midnight celebrations with firecrackers. It falls in the middle of a long holiday period that starts on Christmas Eve and lasts until Epiphany on 6 January. Starting 1 December, there is an annual Christmas Market in Piazza Navona.

Easter is normally a three- or four-day holiday. On Good Friday there's a procession from the Palatine to the Colosseum *(Via Crucis)*, during which the Pope or a high-level cardinal walks the stations of the cross. On Easter Sunday, many people head for St Peter's Square at noon for the Pope's traditional Urbi et Orbi blessing. The saints' days of St Joseph (19 March)

and St John (23 June) are celebrated with special dishes.

The city empties in August when many Romans go on holiday (especially around the Feast of the Assumption on 15 August, referred to as *Ferragosto*), but for the past few years the city council has put on an incredible range of world-class outdoor concerts and other cultural events from June to September, and the city is less deserted than it used to be.

T

TELEPHONES

Several companies provide public payphones, but the most ubiquitous phones are the silver ones run by Telecom, which accept phone cards *(scheda telefonica)* only. You can buy them in various denominations from *tabacchi* and from many newsstands. Some payphones accept credit cards, and many bars have coin-operated payphones. Additionally, there are a number of far cheaper international phone cards available from many newsstands, and there are call centres where you can make your call and pay later, particularly in the area around Stazione Termini.

For a number outside Italy, first dial 00 (the international access code), then the country code, the area code (omitting the initial 0, if applicable) and then the subscriber number.

For international directory enquiries and operator-assisted national and international calls, tel: 892-412.

Calling Rome
Landlines in Rome have an 06 area code which you must use whether calling from within Rome, from outside Rome or from abroad. Numbers in Rome have four to eight digits. Toll-free numbers start with 800.

Mobile phone numbers begin with 3, for example 338, 340, 333, 348, and cost a lot more.

TIME ZONES

Italy follows Central European Time (GMT+1). From the last Sunday in March to the last Sunday in September, clocks are advanced one hour (GMT+2).

TOILETS

Bars are obliged by law to let you use their toilets. This doesn't mean that they will do so with good grace; if you don't spend any money at the bar first they may throw you a look. In many cases bar toilets are locked and you will need to ask for the key *(chiave)* at the till; once inside you may find out that there is no soap or toilet paper. There are now public toilets near most of the major sights and monuments, for which you have to pay a small fee.

TOURIST INFORMATION

The main **Rome Tourist Office** (APT) is at 5 Via Parigi, tel: 06-4889 9200, but it's open to the public only Mon and Thur 9.30am–12.30pm.

The city council offers a **tourism information line** (06 06 08; www. 060608.it) with information in English available from 8am–10pm.

The **Hotel Reservation Service** (in Stazione Termini opposite platform 24, tel: 06-699 1000, www.hotelreserva tion.it; daily 7am–10pm) will make commission-free reservations for you.

The following **tourist information points** or PIT *(punto informativo turistico)* are open daily 9.30am–7.30pm:

- Piazza Pia (Castel Sant'Angelo)
- Piazza del Tempio della Pace (Via dei Fori Imperiali)
- Piazza delle Cinque Lune (Piazza Navona)
- Via Nazionale (Palazzo delle Esposizioni)
- Piazza Sonnino (Trastevere)
- Piazza San Giovanni in Laterano
- Via dell'Olmata (Santa Maria Maggiore)
- Via Marco Minghetti (Trevi Fountain)

There is also an information point in Stazione Termini, in front of platform 4. It opens daily 8am–9pm.

Vatican Tourist Office

The **Vatican Tourist Office** (Ufficio Pellegrini e Turisti) is in Braccio Carlo Magno, Piazza San Pietro (to the left of the basilica), tel: 06-6988 1662 (Mon–Sat 8.30am–6.15pm).

Tourist Information Abroad

Italian State Tourist Office: 1 Princes Street, London W1R 8AY; tel: 020-7408 1254; fax: 020-7493 6695.

Italian Government Tourist Office: 630 Fifth Ave, New York 10111; tel: 212-245 4822; fax: 586-9249.

TOURS

If you want a tour tailored to your needs, Rome is the city to find it.

For classic bus tours with a guide, check out **Carrani Tours** (95 Via Vittorio Emanuele Orlando, tel: 06-474 2501; www.carrani.com) and **Green Line Tours** (5/a Via Farini; tel: 06-482 7480/ 06-482 8647; www.green

linetours.com). For more specialised options, **Nerone** (tel: 339-625 3906 or 773-661 4142 (from the USA); www. nerone.cc) offers Vespa tours, garden walks, and a music tour.

Award-winning author *(As the Romans Do)* and photographer team, Alan and Diane Epstein, offer customized tours and culinary excursions, at www.astheromansdo.com.

TRANSPORT

Arrival by Air

Travellers on scheduled flights land at the main airport, Aeroporto Leonardo da Vinci in Fiumicino, about 30km (18 miles) southwest of Rome (Fiumicino airport, tel: 06-65951). Some flights arrive at Ciampino airport, about 15km (9 miles) to the southeast (Ciampino airport, tel: 06-794 941). From here a bus travels to the Anagnina metro station. For more information, see www.adr.it.

Airport Transport

From Fiumicino airport, trains run to Termini station every 30 minutes until 11.37pm. There is also an infrequent late-night bus service. If you take a taxi, choose only a white one with a meter. Be prepared to pay a taxi fare of around €45–60 (depending on the time of day and how much luggage you have) to your hotel from Fiumicino; €10–20 from Termini or Ostiense. From Ciampino airport, a COTRAL bus runs twice hourly to the Anagnina metro station. Taxis are €25–40 into the city.

A private bus service runs frequently between Ciampino airport and the city in conjunction with Ryanair and easyJet flights (www.terravision. it). For a limousine service, for airport pick-up and tours of Rome, contact Airport Connection Services (tel: 06-338 3221; www.airportconnection.it).

Arrival by Rail

If you are travelling from the UK, note that the cost of a train ticket is, in many cases, a good deal more expensive than the airfare, so it's only worth travelling by train if you have time and money to spare or if you intend to stop off along the way. Most trains arrive at the main Roman station, Termini. Like bus and metro tickets, most train tickets must be validated at a machine in the station before boarding. For routes and reservations: www.trenitalia.it.

Arrival by Bus

If you are travelling by bus both on national or international services, you are likely to arrive on Via Marsala near Termini or the Bus Terminal at Stazione Tiburtina.

Arrival by Road

Car travellers arriving in Rome from any direction first hit the Grande Raccordo Anulare (GRA), the ring motorway. The A1 (Autostrada del Sole) leads into the GRA from both north and south, as does the A24 from the east. If you arrive on the Via del Mare from the coast (Ostia), you can either join the GRA or continue straight into the city centre.

The various roads into the centre lead off the GRA. For the north, choose the exits Via Salaria, Via Flaminia or Via Nomentana. If heading for the Vatican area, follow the GRA to the west and take the exit Via Aurelia. If you're going south, take the Via Tuscolana, Via Appia Nuova, Via Pontina (which leads into the Via Cristoforo Colombo) or the Via del Mare.

When leaving the GRA, follow the white signs to the road you want rather than the blue ones, which usually lead away from the centre. The city-centre sign is a black dot in the middle of a black circle on a white background.

Transport within Rome

Taxis. Meters in white taxis tend to start at around €3. After 10pm, on Sundays and for luggage there is a surcharge. You can order a radio taxi by phone (tel: 06-3570 or 06-6645), which start their meters upon your acceptance (the automated operator will give you an approximate wait time and prompt you to hang up the phone to accept). Fares are some of the highest in Europe, so be prepared to pay.

Buses and trams. Tobacco stores displaying a big 'T' sell metro-tram-bus tickets, without which you are not supposed to board a bus. Tickets are available as: a single ride €1, all-day pass €4, weekly €16, and monthly €30.

Once on board, stamp your ticket in the machine on board. There's a fine of €51 if you're caught without a ticket or without having stamped it. City bus services are operated by Atac (www.atac.roma.it).

The sightseeing Roma (www.roma.city-sightseeing.it) double-decker bus departs regularly from Via Marsala (Termini Station) and does a comprehensive tour of the city. The ticket is good for a full day and allows you get on and off the bus as you please.

Metro. The metro is a skeletal system with only two lines, A and B, intersecting at Termini. It operates daily 5.30am–11.30pm (until 12.30am Saturday). Line A closes daily at 9pm in order for much-needed modernisation work to be carried out. A shuttle bus service (MA1 and MA2) substitutes the stops, but calculate time for traffic. From Piramide, there's a train to Ostia (Ostia Antica and beaches), a stop on the B line metro, and the 23 bus to Trastevere and the Vatican.

For more information and a handy route planner, visit www.atac.roma.it.

Trains. Should you want to leave the city by train, you might find Termini station a frustrating experience with long queues at the enquiries and ticket desks in summer. You are likely to get better service from the city's travel agencies. Tickets must be stamped before boarding at one of the yellow machines dotted around the station.

For more information call 892021 or visit www.trenitalia.com. Tickets can be bought online or by phone, and picked up from one of the many self-service machines dotted around the

station, where you can also buy your tickets directly.

Driving. Driving a car through Rome's tangled streets can be an exercise in frustration. Rental cars are available from: (Avis 06-6501 1531; www.avis autonoleggio.it); Europcar (800-014-410/06-488 2854; www.europcar. com); Hertz (tel: 199-112-211; www. hertz.it); Magiore (tel: 06-6501 0678; www.maggiore.it); Sixt (tel: 199-100-666; www.sixt.com). Most car rental agencies have pick-up points around the city. Save money and hassle by reserving in advance.

If you have the confidence to rent a scooter, call Happy Rent (tel: 06-481 8185; www.happyrent.com). Make sure you are properly insured.

Parking. If driving is a challenge, parking is a downright enigma. While you'll notice little regard for signage on the part of the locals, parking laws do exist. Your best bet is to look for blue painted lines and a large blue 'P'. You can pay by the hour with a machine and leave the receipt in the car.

Parking lots *(parcheggio)* are also marked with a blue 'P' and are staffed by the hour and closed at night. Parcheggio Villa Borghese is the largest, most convenient, and most reliable. Entrance at 33 Viale del Galoppatoio; tel: 06-322-5934; open 24 hours a day.

Petrol. Petrol stations *(benzinaio)* are scattered throughout the city and generally follow business hours. Rates vacillate around €1.50 a litre. For unleaded ask for *senza piombo*. Many stations accept credit cards and all accept cash. If you venture out of the city, you will need cash.

VISAS

EU passport-holders do not require a visa; a valid passport or ID card is sufficient. Visitors from the US, Canada, Australia and New Zealand do not require visas for stays of up to three months; non-EU citizens need a full passport.

Nationals of most other countries do need a visa. This must be obtained in advance from the Italian Consulate.

WEBSITES

• Information on cultural events:
www.whatsoninrome.com
• Vatican Museums:
www.vatican.va
• Official Rome tourist board website:
www.romaturismo.com
• Rome City Council:
www.comune.roma.it
• City Council Tourism:
www.060608.it
• Roman museums:
www.museiincomune.it
• Hotel Reservation Service:
www.hotelreservation.it
• Rome airports:
www.adr.it

Above from far left: lots of scooters zip around the narrow streets; a Fiat 500, the ultimate city car; two wheels are better than four in Rome.

The Forum and Colosseum

Capo d'Africa

54 Via Capo d'Africa; tel: 06-772 801; www.hotelcapodafrica.com; metro: Colosseo; €€€

This hotel's dramatic, palm-tree-lined entrance bodes well, and its 65 rooms are comfortable and contemporary. Views are delightful, especially from the glass-walled rooftop breakfast room.

Celio

35C Via dei Santissimi Quattro; tel: 06-7049 5333; www.hotelcelio.com; metro: Colosseo; €€–€€€

This delightful hotel a few streets from the Colosseum has 20 rooms, named after great Italian artists of the Renaissance, and a lovely rooftop terrace.

Domus Sessoriana

10 Piazza Santa Croce in Gerusalemme; tel: 06-706 151; www.domussessoriana.it; metro: San Giovanni; €€

Attached to the monastery of the church next door, this hotel offers simple, elegant accommodation. Request a room overlooking the monastery's garden.

Hotel 47

47 Via Petroselli; tel: 06-678 7816; www.47hotel.com; bus: 170
€€€–€€€€

This plush modern hotel is set in an austere 1930s building which has been tastefully converted and filled with repro furniture and contemporary artworks. The views are wonderful, especially from the rooftop restaurant.

Inn at the Roman Forum

30 Via degli Ibernesi; tel: 06-6919 0970; www.theinnattheromanforum.com; bus: 75; €€€–€€€€

This new boutique hotel offers luxurious rooms with canopied beds, antique furnishings, a prime location and even its own ancient Roman crypt.

Lancelot

47 Via Capo d'Africa; tel: 06-7045 0615; www.lancelothotel.com; metro: Colosseo; €€

This ultra-friendly, family-run hotel has light, airy rooms and enjoys an enviable position, a few minutes' walk from the Colosseum.

Trevi Fountain and Quirinale

Daphne Trevi

20 Via degli Avignonesi, Trevi; tel: 06-8745 0087; www.daphne-rome.com; metro: Barberini; €€

This hotel offers excellent service – friendly, knowledgeable staff, and laptops (one per floor) and mobile phones (one per room) provided.

Residenza Cellini

5 Via Modena; tel: 06-4782 5204; www.residenzacellini.it; metro: Repubblica; €€–€€€

Prices for an average double room in high season:	
€€€€	€350 and above
€€€	€180–350
€€	€100–180
€	under €100

With rooms that are unusually large for the price, this hotel is deservedly popular. The decor is classic, with parquet floors, wood furnishings and fabrics in flouncy florals.

Casa Howard

18 Via Capo le Case and 149 Via Sistina; tel: 06-6992 4555; www.casahoward.com; metro: Spagna; €€–€€€

Each of the 10 rooms in this stylish hotel in two locations has a different theme; those in the newer Via Sistina location are slightly more luxurious.

Gregoriana

18 Via Gregoriana; tel: 06-679 4269; www.hotelgregoriana.it; metro: Spagna; €€

Fans of Art Deco will adore the striking retro interior of this ex-convent, with its wonderful lift and original 1930s room numbers by the Russian fashion designer Erté.

Hotel Art

56 Via Margutta; tel: 06-328 711; www.hotelart.it; metro: Spagna; €€€€

Set in a converted seminary, this upmarket hotel blends old and new. The reception area is within two futuristic pods, while the sleek lounge area is beneath frescoed vaulted ceilings.

Inn at the Spanish Steps

85 Via dei Condotti; tel: 06-6992 5657; www.atspanishsteps.com; metro: Spagna; €€–€€€€

The stunning rooms at this luxury boutique hotel are a mix of carefully selected antiques and bold fabrics; some boast 17th-century frescoes.

Modigliani

42 Via della Purificazione; tel: 06-4281 5226; www.hotelmodigliani.com; metro: Spagna; €€

A lovely hotel with great views from top-floor rooms and a garden in an inner courtyard.

Pensione Panda

35 Via della Croce; tel: 06-678 0179; www.hotelpanda.it; metro: Spagna; €

A rare budget option a stone's throw from the Spanish Steps, its rooms, though small and basic, have been attractively decorated.

Suisse

54 Via Gregoriana; tel: 06-678 3649; www.hotelsuisserome.com; metro: Spagna; €€

This charming hotel has large rooms, parquet floors and classic decor. Breakfast is served in the rooms. Great value.

Bramante

24 Vicolo delle Palline; tel: 06-6880 6426; www.hotelbramante.com; metro: Ottaviano; €€

This 15th-century former inn on a tranquil side street near St Peter's is now a charming hotel. The small terrace makes a pleasant place to unwind after a busy day.

Above from far left: detail from a room in Hotel Celio; breakfast at Hotel Art and one of the hotel's reception pods; lobby at Celio.

Hotel Options

Traditionally Rome has always been an expensive city to stay in, with price often a poor reflection of quality. In recent years the accommodation options have begun to broaden so that, while still expensive, you can now choose to avoid the peeling pensione of old. Conventional facades now hide avant-garde interiors, while at the grander end of the scale, gracious, timeless hotels retain their cachet. But for those not on an imperial budget there are plenty of welcoming guesthouses and family-run hotels, while self-catering apartments and bed and breakfasts are increasingly popular options.

Cavalieri Hilton

101 Via Cadlolo; tel: 06-350 91; www.cavalieri-hilton.it; bus: 991; €€€€

Luxury hotel just north of the Vatican. Quiet and spacious, it has tennis courts and swimming pools, as well as one of Rome's best restaurants, La Pergola.

Colors

31 Via Boezio; tel: 06-687 4030; www.colorshotel.com; metro: Ottaviano; €–€€

Bright, clean hotel, with rooms with or without en suite bathroom, and dormitory accommodation. Kitchen, laundry facilities and a roof terrace.

Farnese

30 Via Alessandro Farnese; tel: 06-321 2553; www.hotelfarnese.com; bus: 70; €€–€€€

This upmarket 4-star hotel occupies a grand old aristocratic residence. Rooms are elegant with antiques, marble bathrooms and Murano lamps. The breakfast is excellent, and there is a pretty roof terrace.

Franklin

29 Via Rodi; tel: 06-3903 0165; www.franklinhotelrome.it; metro: Ottaviano; €€–€€€

This modern hotel has airy, pleasant rooms, all with a musical theme. There's music for guests to borrow, plus bicycles for guests' use.

Sant'Anna

133 Borgo Pio; tel: 06-6880 1602; www.hotelsantanna.com; metro: Ottaviano; €€

Housed in a 16th-century building, this hotel has comfortable rooms with a slightly old-fashioned feel. Breakfast is taken in the small courtyard at the back or the mural-decorated breakfast room. Service is friendly.

Piazza Navona and the Pantheon

Due Torri

23 Vicolo del Leonetto, off Via dell'Orso; tel: 06-6880 6956; www.hotelduetorriroma.com; bus: 70; €€

A delightful hotel – in a former cardinal's palace tucked away down a narrow cobbled street – and quiet by Roman standards.

Navona

8 Via dei Sediari; tel: 06-686 4203; www.hotelnavona.com; bus: 64; €€

This family-run hotel on the second floor of an attractive palazzo was built on the site of the ancient baths of Agrippa – the ground floor dates back to AD 1. Good value for the location.

Raphael

2 Largo Febo, off Piazza Navona; tel: 06-682 831; www.raphael hotel.com; bus: 116; €€€€

A distinctive ivy-covered exterior, antique furnishings, artworks and

Prices for an average double room in high season:	
€€€€	€350 and above
€€€	€180–350
€€	€100–180
€	under €100

Above from far left: Hotel Eden's elegant lobby.

stunning views. Some rooms don't quite live up to expectations, but the rooftop restaurant, bar and views do.

Relais Palazzo Taverna

92 Via dei Gabrielli; tel: 06-2039 8064; www.relaispalazzo taverna.com; bus: 70; €€

Rooms at this smart new guesthouse have stylish, modern decor, with tiled floors and frescoes. Excellent value.

Teatro Pace 33

33 Via del Teatro Pace; tel: 06-6879 075; www.hotelteatropace.com; bus: 40; €€

This 17th-century building on a quiet backstreet, has a magnificent Baroque spiral staircase (there's no lift) and wood-beamed rooms decorated in classic style, with marble bathrooms.

Campo de' Fiori and the Ghetto

Barrett

47 Largo Torre Argentina; tel: 06-686 8481; www.pensione barrett.com; bus: 40; €€

This great-value hotel has been run by the same family for over 40 years. The knick-knacks and quirky antiques which cram every room provide character. No credit cards.

Campo de' Fiori

6 Piazza del Biscione; tel: 06-6880 6865; www.hotelcampodefiori.com; bus: 64; €€

This hotel has a beautiful roof terrace and intimate, individually decorated rooms with bijou en suite bathrooms.

Ponte Sisto

64 Via dei Pettinari; tel: 06-686 310; www.hotelpontesisto.it; bus: 23; €€–€€€

Once the residence of a noble Venetian family, the rooms here are elegant and simple, with luxurious marble bathrooms. The courtyard is a pleasant spot for an early evening aperitivo.

Teatro di Pompeo

8 Largo del Pallaro; tel: 06-6830 0170; www.hotelteatrodipompeo.it; bus: 116; €€

This charming, friendly hotel was built on the site of the ancient Theatre of Pompey (the remains of which can still be seen in the vaulted breakfast room).

Via Veneto and Villa Borghese

Aldrovandi Palace

15 Via Ulisse Aldrovandi; tel: 06-322 3993; www.aldrovandi.com; bus: M; €€€€

Sumptuous rooms and suites at this beautiful hotel. The lovely gardens, spectacular outdoor pool and restaurant (Baby), run by a Michelin-starred chef, are further draws.

Eden

49 Via Ludovisi; tel: 06-478 121; www.starwoodhotels.com; bus: 116; €€€€

This discreet, ultra-refined hotel rejects ostentatious opulence in favour of classic, pared-down elegance. Excellent, un-snooty service, and a gourmet roof garden restaurant, La Terrazza dell' Eden, with views to die for.

Historic Centre

Rome offers countless places to stay, but the area around Piazza Navona, the Pantheon and Campo de' Fiori offers perhaps the best introduction to the city, since you are right in its medieval heart and within easy reach of most main sights. However, there are relatively few hotels in the area, and these tend to be booked up early, so try to plan ahead if possible.

Lord Byron

5 Via Giuseppe de Notaris; tel: 06-322 0404; www.lordbyronhotel.com; bus: 52; €€€–€€€€

Built into a former monastery, this small hotel has the atmosphere of a private club, and enjoys a serene location away from the city centre.

Westin Excelsior

125 Via Vittorio Veneto; tel: 06-47081; www.starwood.com; metro: Barberini; €€€€

Part of the 1950s dolce vita scene and always the grandest of Via Veneto's 5-stars, the Excelsior offers the ultimate in opulence and glamour, with staggeringly luxurious, antiques-laden rooms.

Trastevere and the Gianicolo

Antico Borgo Trastevere

7 Vicolo del Buco; tel: 06-588 3774; www.hotelanticoborgo.it; bus: H; €–€€

In a pleasant location on the quieter, eastern side of Trastevere, this budget hotel's rooms are for the most part tiny, but tastefully decorated. Breakfast is served at nearby sister hotel the Domus Tiberina, on a piazza overlooking the river.

Arco del Lauro

27 Via dell'Arco de' Tolomei, off Via del Salumi; tel: 06-9784 0350; www.arcodellauro.it; bus: 125; €€

Mini-hotel, with just four rooms, in a tranquil part of Trastevere. Fresh, simple and excellent-value rooms Breakfast is served in a nearby bar.

Residenza Arco de' Tolomei

26C Via dell'Arco de' Tolomei; tel: 06-5832 0819; www.inrome.info; bus: 125; €€

On a quiet alley with just five rooms, three with terraces. Decorated in country-house style, with a homely feel. Breakfast is a real event here, with homemade baked goods and jams served in a light-filled breakfast room.

San Francesco

7 Via Jacopa de' Settesoli; tel: 06-5830 0051; www.hotelsanfrancesco.net; bus: 44; €€

Set back a little from the bustle of central Trastevere, rooms are good-sized and comfortable; ask for one of the rooms overlooking the internal courtyard of the adjacent convent. Breakfast is served on the roof terrace in warm weather.

Santa Maria

2 Vicolo del Piede; tel: 06-589 4626; www.htlsantamaria.com; bus: H; €€

Gated, refurbished 16th-century cloister. Rooms are large and comfortable, with a view out onto a large, sunny central courtyard planted with orange trees. Bikes are available for guests' use. One room has been adapted for people with disabilities.

Prices for an average double room in high season:	
€€€€	€350 and above
€€€	€180–350
€€	€100–180
€	under €100

Trastevere

24A–25 Via L. Manara; tel: 06-581 4713; www.hoteltrastevere.net; bus: H; €–€€

With clean, simple rooms overlooking Piazza San Cosimato market square, this charming, down-to-earth little hotel is a great deal for the area, with good-value apartments for rent nearby.

Aventino, Testaccio and EUR

Sant'Anselmo

2 Piazza Sant'Anselmo; tel: 06-570 057; www.aventinohotels.com; metro: Circo Massimo; €€–€€€

Nestling in a peaceful garden on the exclusive Aventine Hill, each room in this hotel has been given its own imaginative theme. Four-poster beds, free-standing baths and frescoes make it a very special place to stay.

Villa San Pio

19 Via di Santa Melania; tel: 06-570 057; www.aventinohotels.com; metro: Circo Massimo; €€

This hotel consists of three separate buildings which share the same attractive gardens. It has elegant, spacious rooms with antique furnishings and generous bathrooms with jacuzzis.

Celio, Monti and Esquilino

Des Artistes

20 Via Villafranca, off Via Vicenza; tel: 06-445 4365; www.hoteldes artistes.com; metro: Termini; €

Quality of accommodation tends to dip around the station, but this is an exception: though the rooms are simple, they're comfortable and clean, and staff are friendly and helpful.

The Beehive

8 Via Marghera; tel: 06-4470 4553; www.the-beehive.com; metro: Termini; €

Rooms at this appealing budget option all have shared bathroom, but are clean and stylishly decorated. There's also a small organic restaurant, a yoga space and a sunny patio.

Exedra

47 Piazza della Repubblica; tel: 06-489 381; www.boscolohotels.com; metro: Repubblica; €€€€

Among the most opulent of the city's 5-star hotels, the Exedra is glamorous, with luxurious, no-expense-spared rooms and stunning suites that are a favourite with visiting film stars.

Montreal

4 Via Carlo Alberto; tel: 06-445 7797; www.hotelmontrealrome.com; metro: Termini; €€

The Montreal's 27 rooms are bright, cheery and spacious, and its small, flower-filled patio makes a lovely spot for breakfast in the summer months.

Radisson SAS Hotel

171 Via Filippo Turati; tel: 06-444 841; www.radissonsas.com; metro: Termini; €€€

This cutting-edge-design hotel has a spectacular rooftop terrace with a restaurant and a pool (in summer). Its location opposite the station is convenient but far from picturesque.

Above from far left: suite in the Westin Excelsior; hidden away down this alley in Trastevere is lovely Hotel Santa Maria; the Excelsior's grand facade on Via Veneto.

APT List
The APT office publishes an annual list (Annuario Alberghi) showing star categories, facilities and prices of all Rome hotels. This may be obtained from the APT or through Italian national tourist offices: Rome Tourist Office APT; 5 Via Parigi; tel: 06-488 991.

The Forum and Colosseum

Caffé Martini

Piazza del Colosseo 3; tel: 06-700 4431; Mon–Sat; €

There are several little cafés with outdoor tables looking directly at the Colosseum. This is the best for food and price in the area. Here you'll find a decent lunch service and good pizza in the evening.

Gelateria Ara Coeli

Piazza Ara Coeli 10; tel: 06-679 5085; 11am–9pm; €

This is a great gelateria just near the steps to the Capitoline Hill. In addition to their homemade gelato (including the deepest, darkest and most delicious chocolate fondant ice cream) they also have sugarless and milk-free versions.

Hostaria Nerone

Via delle Terme di Tito 96; tel: 06-481 7952; Tue–Sun lunch and dinner; €–€€

A classic osteria that serves up great home cooking, with views overlooking the Colosseum. Their antipasto, oxtail stew and veal are all excellent. The best choice for atmosphere and quality in the area.

Price guide for a two-course meal for one with half a bottle of house wine.

€€€€	€60 and above
€€€	€40–60
€€	€25–40
€	under €25

Ristorante Mario's

Piazza del Grillo 9; tel: 06-679 3725; Tue–Sun noon–3pm, 6.30–11pm; €–€€

Traditional Roman food served (fish is their speciality) at surprisingly affordable prices in this touristy area. Informal at lunchtimes, more elegant for dinner; with a lovely pergola in the square outside.

San Teodoro

Via dei Fienili 49–51; tel: 06-678 0933; Mon–Sat noon–3pm, 6.30–11pm; €€€€

Located in a tranquil piazza, this elegant restaurant stands out in a non-foodie part of town. It offers traditional dishes creatively updated and centred on seasonal availability. Staples are fish carpaccios and delicious homemade pasta.

Trevi Fountain and Quirinale

Al Moro

Vicolo delle Bollette 13; tel: 06-678 3495; Mon–Sat 7.30–11.30pm; €€€

Located just a few minutes from the Trevi Fountain is this old favourite with the local boutique owners and Via dei Condotti shoppers. The menu is classic, with Roman pastas and artichokes, but with a twist – also featuring Sicilian fish dishes such as swordfish and calamari, and fish carpaccio.

Il Gelato di San Crispino

Via della Panetteria 42; tel: 06-679 3925; Fri–Wed noon–12.30am; €

Above from far left: pizza is a Roman staple; wine for sale; the basis of many a pasta dish; tables in a trattoria.

The handmade gelato served here – in paper cups rather than cones, which are said to contaminate the flavour – is thought by some to be the best in the country, let alone the city. Try the honey-flavoured San Crispino, sesame or dark chocolate.

Le Colline Emiliane

Via degli Avignonesi 22; tel: 06-481 7538; Mon–Sat 8–11.30pm; €€€

This lovely restaurant, which is situated just near the Palazzo Barberini, serves up mouthwatering dishes from the Emilia-Romagna region. Their northern-style sauces and stewed or grilled meats are a wonderful change to typical, ubiquitous pasta dishes.

Piccolo Arancio

Via Scanderbeg 112; tel: 06-678 6139; Tue–Sun noon–3pm, 7–midnight; €€

Sit for lunch or dinner at this restaurant's charming outdoor tables just behind the Quirinale, and order speciality dishes like ravioli with an orange and ricotta filling, or creamy risotto with radicchio.

Vineria Il Chianti

Via del Lavatore 81; tel: 06-679 2470; daily noon–2am; €€

Just around the corner from the Trevi Fountain is this cute Tuscan wine bar with decent food. They serve Florentine steaks and pasta with a wild boar sauce, plus a great selection of Chianti.

Piazza di Spagna and Tridente

Dal Bolognese

Piazza del Popolo 1; tel: 06-361 1426; Tue–Sun dinner only; €€€

This classic restaurant is elegant but not stuffy and has returning clientele that include celebrities and models. The menu is also traditional with - unsurprisingly - favourites such as pasta Bolognese and a tortellini soup. They serve an excellent selection of shellfish dishes, and expensive but good wines.

Il Margutta

Via Margutta 118; tel: 06-3265 0577; Mon–Sat lunch and dinner, €€–€€€

A vegetarians' haven in the middle of lamb-loving Rome, where you'll find excellently prepared creative dishes, and versions of classic favourites.

Matricianella

Via del Leone 4; tel: 06-683 2100; Mon–Sat noon–3pm and 7.30–11pm; €€

This place is so popular with locals that it must be good. Classic Roman dishes are served in a bustling atmosphere where the decor is akin to an Italian grandmother's kitchen. To start, try their crispy *fritti* (deep fried vegetables, courgette flowers and morsels of meat in batter) and then perhaps the *abbacchio al forno*, roast suckling lamb.

Otello alla Concordia

Via delle Croce 81; tel: 06-679 1178; Mon–Sat dinner; €€

Un Caffè

Coffee is serious business in Italy. It is often social but not something to linger over, and has its own etiquette. A basic coffee is a caffè (espresso), which can be adjusted by the addition of hot water for an americano, or varying amounts of steamed or frothed milk such as in a cappuccino or caffè latte. Milky coffees are considered breakfast drinks and are very rarely ordered after 11am. A caffè macchiato (stained coffee) is the appropriate replacement, consisting of an espresso with a dash of milk froth.

The Concordia is a simple, traditional Roman osteria located in the middle of a trendy dining area. They serve all the Roman classics such as *pasta all'amitriciana* (spicy red sauce flavoured with pork cheek), *cacio e pepe (see margin, right)*, and gnocchi, with seasonal vegetables, and freshly baked cakes.

Benito e Gilberto al Falco

Via del Falco 19; tel: 06-686 7769; Tue–Sat 7.30pm–1am; €€€

This is a seafood lover's delight. Nearly every dish is fish-based and only the freshest is served. Photos on the wall testify to the many celebrities who have eaten here.

Il Matriciano

Via dei Gracchi 55; tel: 06-321 3040; noon–3.30pm, 7.30–11pm; €

A typical neighbourhood trattoria with local businessmen and families dining here. Excellent standard fare and Roman classics, away from the Vatican crowds. *Pasta all'amatriciana* is the house dish.

Ristro

Via della Conciliazione 2; tel: 06-683 92127; 8am–11pm; €

Price guide for a two-course meal for one with half a bottle of house wine.

€€€€	€60 and above
€€€	€40–60
€€	€25–40
€	under €25

This no-frills eatery has plenty of well-lit and modern tables, and serves a large selection of food all day. It will not be the best meal you have in Rome but it is strategically located between the Vatican and the Castel Sant'Angelo.

Maccheroni

Piazza delle Coppelle 44; tel: 06-6830 7895; 1–3pm, 8pm–12.30am; €€

Simple pasta dishes, seasonal greens, roast lamb and excellent desserts are served in a former butcher's shop. Always a popular spot in the centre of the city.

Myosotis

Via della Vaccarella 3; tel: 06-686 5554; Mon–Sat 12.30–3.30pm, 7–11.30pm; €€

The focus here is on local produce and fresh fish. Wonderfully prepared meats, grilled vegetables and specialities like liver and tripe are served in a cute piazza, with a great wine list.

Obika

Via dei Prefetti 26; tel: 06-683 2630; Mon–Sat; 12.30–4pm, 8–11pm; €€€

Rome may be the only city to offer cheese as a main dish. Obika means 'here it is!' in the Neapolitan dialect, and this place has it. A foodie heaven, Obika is modern with a menu dedicated to multiple types of fresh mozzarella. They offer side dishes and great wines to accompany the cheese.

Salotto 42

Piazza di Pietra 42; tel: 06-678 504;
Tue–Sun; €€

A lovely bar with low tables, art books
and velvet cushions also serves breakfast with fresh baked goods, a mean
evening appetiser, and a la carte dishes. A beautiful setting for the beautiful people.

Supperclub

Via dei Nari 14; tel: 06-6880 7207;
8pm–2am; €€€

There is no menu, and dinner is
brought out in courses to your 'bed'.
Prices are fixed, with a separate wine
list. It is a slow dining experience
accompanied by performances and a
DJ spinning dinner music, changing
to a club atmosphere after 11pm.
Reservations are necessary.

Campo de' Fiori and the Ghetto

Al Bric

Via del Pellegrino 51; tel: 06-687
9533; 12.30–11.30pm; €€€

This little place has walls decorated
with wine labels and boxes, and has
one of the best wine lists in the city.
To go with the great wines they offer
a large selection of unusual cheeses
and creative pasta dishes with interesting sauces. The bread and the cakes
are freshly baked.

Fileti di Baccalà

Largo di Librari 88; tel: 06-686
4018; Mon–Sat 6–11pm; €

This is the Roman version of a fish
and chip shop. Golden pieces of bat-
tered and fried salt cod are wrapped in
paper and served with sautéed cour-
gettes and beer. There is outdoor seating on the piazza in summer.

Il Giardino Romano

Via del Portico di Ottavia 13; tel: 06-
6880 9661; daily 12.30–11.30pm;
€€

This popular combination of pizzeria
and trattoria is located next to several
other restaurants in the Ghetto. Il Giardino has the advantage of outdoor
seating in their cool walled garden
located at the back. The menu includes
favourites such as Jewish fried artichokes, and specials like fettuccine
with grilled sea bass or ravioli with a
creamy orange zest sauce.

Osteria Romana

Via di San Paolo alla Regola 29; tel:
06-686 1917; Tue–Sun; €€€€

This is a charming place located on
a side piazza. Mountains of vegetables and appetisers greet your
arrival. Their speciality dish is
grilled fish in paper. The understated elegance has been a favourite of
visiting dignitaries.

Piperno

Via Monte de'Cenci 9; tel: 06-683
3606; Tue–Sun 12.45–2.30pm,
Tue–Sat 8–10.30pm; €€€

One of the oldest restaurants in the
Ghetto, up and running since 1860.
This lovely trattoria serves many typical Roman Jewish dishes, such as
fried artichoke and sweetbreads, and
baked fish.

**Above from far
left:** outside tables
in Piazza Navona;
peppers; artichokes
are a Roman
favourite; in an
enoteca (wine bar)

Typical Dishes
Roman cuisine is
based on good
hearty dishes and
meats. Most menus
will include some
version of pasta
with a salty pecor-
ino cheese, like
cacio e pepe
(cheese and freshly
ground black
pepper), *spaghetti
all'amatriciana*
(spicy tomato sauce
with *guanciale*, a
salt pork taken from
the cheek), and
pasta carbonara
(creamy egg and
cheese sauce
seasoned with
guanciale). Other
favourites are
carciofi giudaio
(whole fried arti-
chokes) and *fiori di
zucca* (fried cour-
gette with cheese
and anchovy).

Ciampini

Viale Trinitá dei Monti; tel: 06-678 5678; 12.30–11.30pm; €€

This restaurant provides a great place to relax with views, cool breezes and atmosphere. It is an affordable choice on the Pincio. Perfect for before or after a day at the Villa Borghese.

La Terrazza at Eden

Via Ludovisi 49; tel: 06-4781 2752; dinner; €€€€

La Terrazza in the Hotel Eden is considered the most romantic view in Rome. The hushed environment, perfect service and succulent dishes add up to an unforgettable, if expensive, meal. Jacket and tie, and reservations, are essential.

Papa Baccus

Via Toscana 36; tel: 06-4274 2808; dinner; Mon–Sat 12.30–3.30pm, 8–11.30pm; €€€

Giving a great twist to Tuscan classics, with a genuinely seasonal menu, this place is very popular. They breed their own pigs, ensuring the freshest cuts and sausages.

Price guide for a two-course meal for one with half a bottle of house wine.

€€€€	€60 and above
€€€	€40–60
€€	€25–40
€	under €25

Checco er Carettiere

Via Benedetta 10; tel: 06-581 7018; Tue–Sun dinner; €€

A beloved and well-worn trattoria with a classic Trastevere feel. This popular place is always packed, and the menu caters to the hearty Roman worker with the classics. Homely, filling and really authentic. They have a surprisingly decent selection of local wines.

Il Boom

Via dei Fienaroli 31; tel: 06-589 7169; Tue–Sun dinner; €€

A popular spot for both atmosphere and food. The walls here are decorated with film posters and the décor has a 1960s retro feel. Their menu is good and the food is consistently well prepared. Live jazz is often played after dinner.

Glass

Vicolo del Cinque 58; tel: 06-5833 5903; daily; €€€

In the middle of a sea of traditional pizzerie and old world pasta eateries, Glass adds a modern twist. Clean lines and contemporary style match the unusually creative menu with blueberry sauces for the meats and cheese gelato with fruit as an appetiser.

Roma Sparita

Piazza Santa Cecilia 24; tel: 06-580 0757; Tue–Sun 12.30–4pm, 7.30–11.30pm; €€

A good choice for a lazy lunch after wandering the streets of Trastevere.

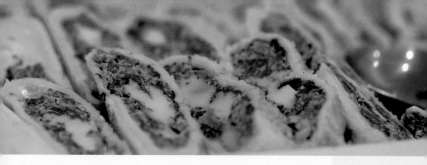

Both the price and location have made this osteria popular for generations. Their menu has all of the Roman classics, and they serve the *cacio e pepe* in a basket made of toasted parmesan.

Aventino and Testaccio

Da Oio a Casa Mia

Via Galvani 43; tel: 06-578 2680; Tue–Sun dinner; €€

An unpretentious family-run trattoria with bags of atmosphere serving up classic pasta dishes in rich meaty sauces. If you like offal, try the *rigatoni alla pajata* (baby lamb's intestines).

Perilli

Via Marmorata 39; tel: 06-574 2415; Thur–Tue lunch and dinner; €€€

Perilli has been in business for nearly 100 years, happily serving long relaxed dinners in Roman style. The outdated interior and bow-tied waiters add charm and nostalgia. Pastas are tossed tableside, and they specialize in meats cut and cooked in a hundred ways (it was once a stone's throw from the main slaughterhouse and butchers). Complete the meal with a local wine and freshly baked tortes.

Celio, Monti and Esquilino

Agata e Romeo

Via Carlo Alberto 45; tel: 06-446 6115; Mon–Fri 7.30–11pm; €€€€

One of Rome's best treasures. Understated charm is paired with some of the best food in the country. While the menu looks very traditional the award-winning chef Agata Parisello adds her own special touch to the delicate sauces and seasonings. The food is cooked and served to perfection. There are a limited number of tables, and they often close to the public for visiting royalty and dignitaries. Reservations are obligatory; book well in advance.

FISH

Via dei Serpenti 16; tel: 06-24962; Tue–Sun 7pm–midnight; €€€

This fish restaurant is modern with a surprising Asian fusion twist. The oyster bar is perfect for cocktails, and the menu has an excellent selection of seafood dishes.

La Cicala e la Formica

Via Leonina 17; tel: 06-481 7490; Tue–Sun; €€

In the heart of Monti is this tiny little trattoria with a handful of tables on the street. They serve fresh made pastas and a number of seasonal dishes. The vegetables and fish are from the local market.

Trattoria Monti

Via di San Vito 13; tel: 06-446 6573; Tue–Sun 12.30–3.30pm, 7.30–11.30pm; €€–€€€

A few years ago this local trattoria, with friendly service, crisp linens and great food, was a hidden gem. It has been 'discovered' now but the quality and style remain. The basis of the menu is cusine from the east coast and Le Marche region, with an extensive wine list. Reservations are recommended.

Food on the Go
Romans love a leisurely meal, but stopping for a slice of pizza (*pizza a taglio*), a few scoops of ice cream or a shot of shaved ice with syrup (*grattachecca*) is all part of the pleasure of the *passeggiata* or evening stroll.

CREDITS

Insight Step by Step Rome
Written by: Éowyn Kerr and
Annie B. Shapero
Edited by: Alex Knights
Series Editor: Clare Peel
Cartography Editors: Zoë Goodwin and
James Macdonald
Picture Manager: Steven Lawrence
Art Editor: Ian Spick
Production: Kenneth Chan
Photography by: Apa: Britta Jaschinski,
Anna Mockford & Nick Bonetti, Bill Wassman,
Alessandra Santarelli, except akg-Images 20T;
The Bridgeman Art Library 7BR, 21T, 60T;
Fotolibra 2–3; istock photo 15BR, 18/19, 34/35,
34BL, 94TL, 96T; Leonardo 112TL, 112TR,
113TR, 114/115T, 116TL, 117TR; courtesy of
Casale Cento Corvi 92BL, 92/93T.
Cover: main image: Fridmar Damm/Corbis;
bottom left and right: istock photo.

Printed by: Insight Print Services (Pte) Ltd,
38 Joo Koon Road, Singapore 628990

First Edition 2008

DISTRIBUTION

Worldwide
**Apa Publications GmbH & Co. Verlag KG
(Singapore branch)**, 38 Joo Koon Road,
Singapore 628990
Tel: (65) 6865 1600
Fax: (65) 6861 6438

UK and Ireland
GeoCenter International Ltd
Meridian House, Churchill Way West,
Basingstoke, Hampshire, RG21 6YR
Tel: (44) 01256 817 987
Fax: (44) 01256 817 988

United States
Langenscheidt Publishers, Inc.
36–36 33rd Street, 4th Floor,
Long Island City, NY 11106
Tel: (1) 718 784 0055
Fax: (1) 718 784 0640

Australia
Universal Publishers
1 Waterloo Road, Macquarie Park, NSW 2113
Tel: (61) 2 9857 3700
Fax: (61) 2 9888 9074

New Zealand
Hema Maps New Zealand Ltd (HNZ)
Unit D, 24 Ra ORA Drive,
East Tamaki, Auckland
Tel: (64) 9 273 6459
Fax: (64) 9 273 6479

CONTACTING THE EDITORS

We would appreciate it if readers would alert us
to errors or outdated information by writing to
us at insight@apaguide.co.uk or Apa Publications,
PO Box 7910, London SE1 1WE, UK.

www.insightguides.com

INDEX

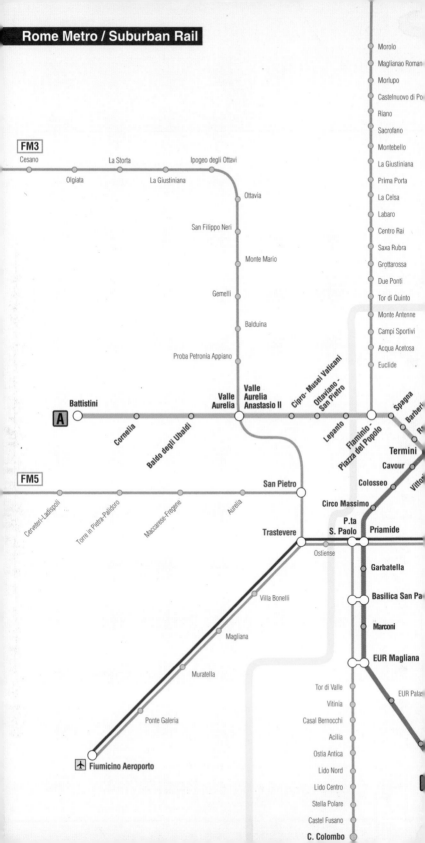